# You Deserve the Best

## How to stop self sabotage and deserve more

---

**Pat Pearson M.S.S.W.**


**Connemara Press**
**8350 Meadow Rd. Suite 284**
**Dallas, Texas 75231**

# TABLE OF CONTENTS

Pearson, Patricia 1950 -
You Deserve The Best: How To Stop Self Sabotage And Deserve More.

Includes index
ISBN- 0-9629462-0-6

1. Psychology 2. Business 3. Success 4. Self Help

Published by
Connemara Press
8350 Meadow, Suite 284
Dallas, Texas 75231

# Acknowledgments

This book has been cooking for five years, in that time many chefs have added their personal spice. I am so grateful for all the love and encouragement that I have received. The support of friends invited me to "Deserve" this book and nurtured me in those moments I was tempted to throw up my hands and give up.

John McCormick for his insight and loving direction. Susan Ellis, my dearest friend and soul sister for her unfailing belief in me. Jim Logan who believed in me a long time before I did and holds the title of oldest of my friends . Ann and Fred Margolin, my dear friends, who edited, inspired and teased me through this process.

Helen Hunt and Harville Hendrix for being my literary and personal beacons in a dark night

Peter McGugan who spans all categories - friend, author, supporter and cosmic connector.

None of us reach our dreams without kind hands pointing the way or shielding us from the wrong paths. My literary pathfinders were my adopted mother and mentor, Vivian Castleberry, David Marquis and the invincible Roz Van Meter. Roz's special gift of joy and brilliance are so wonderfully integrated that they shine in all she does. This book owes her a great tribute.

There is one person who has contributed so consistently and substantially to me that without her my life wouldn't begin to work. Dianne Dobbs, my director of sales, personal friend and constant cheerleader.

In the full circle of life, I begin and end with my family of origin. My father, Winston Pearson, my brothers Tim and Scott. Through all the years the bond grows and develops and we all deserve more.

Finally, I dedicate this book to two wonderful women. My mother, Phyllis Pearson, a bright star on both my personal and professional stage. My first glimpses of joy and deserving were seen in her eyes. Her lightness of heart and largeness of spirit became all that's good in me. I miss her and treasure the love that's between us.

Charlene Calvert, my dear friend who loved deeply and shared generously with me for many years of her life.

# Prologue

## My Sabotage Strategy

I guess it's inevitable that whatever I write about, I live — but I'm sick and tired of sabotaging myself in regard to this book. It has been a dream of mine for years. I've thought about it, written many drafts, been mad at it, loved it — the whole emotional shooting match. What I haven't done is finish it.

It has become a surrogate child, as any form of creativity does, and it has taken on a life of its own. Right now I think it has entered its troubled, tumultuous adolescence.

Every time I sit down to complete it, something, someone (all of them me), sabotages the completion. I get sick or become overly tired or have an emotional crisis, or worse, I start to clean house instead of writing.

Pure, unadulterated sabotage. What's wrong with me? I want to finish, I truly want this five-year dream realized. As many of my clients say, "I really want to be successful, so why do I limit myself?" Or, "I want a good, loving relationship. Why do I choose people who aren't interested?"

Good questions. The answers aren't easy or obvious. We all want the very best for ourselves. I have never met anyone who said, "Just give me the leftovers. I'll take second best." We want the best but don't always achieve or even permit it. Why?

Obviously, some of the why's of our not living up to our potential are out of our control. Acts of God, stockmarket dips, real estate failures, the personal decisions of others. That leaves those reasons which are our own responsibility.

Most of our reasons for self-limitation are created and enforced within ourselves. From our histories and experiences, we lack permission to have what we want. From our own inner wars, we lack the courage to take a risk into our emotional unknown.

Fears can rule us and limit our successes.

If that is true, and I do believe it is, what is my fear that is stopping me from finishing this book?

Reviewing one's own fears is always a hazardous job, but here goes. This book and the impact

I hope it will make are tremendously important to me. I want to get it right. So over and over again I write, rewrite, worry about this phrase or that and generally drive myself crazy.

This perfectionistic part of me is a fatal flaw. It exhausts my creativity and makes me see only what is wrong with the book. That is one of my sabotage messages: "If I do it, I have to do it perfectly." So, I subtly choose to avoid doing it at all.

An even deeper sabotage may be, "What if I pour my heart, soul, and fifteen years of psychological work into this book and no one likes it?"

"What if it's (I'm) not good enough?" The fear of failure or rejection is a very powerful fear of mine, and maybe of yours too. I reject myself, and my desires to create a book, in order to avoid possible rejection or failure. Not a very effective or fun lifestyle.

As I write out all these fears they start to shrink, and an amazing experience happens. I feel better, freer. Somehow a weight has been lifted. Whatever the outcome of writing this book, I am committed to finishing the process. For no other reason than it's my dream, I deserve to play it out to its completion.

Don't you deserve the same?

# •1•

# Sabotage War Stories: The Art of Shooting Yourself in the Foot

*"Argue for your limitations, and sure enough, they're yours."*

*Richard Bach, Illusions*

As a psychotherapist I spent many years talking with people about the deep, heartfelt issues of their lives. I shared their tears, laughter, and dreams. I also shared my own.

As I was driving home one night, I reflected on all the many issues and personal problems I had heard that day. Where was the thread? What was the universal song that everyone was singing?

I decided that it boiled down to this. We all wanted the best for ourselves — no one wished for financial problems or health concerns or bad relationships. We wanted the best, but many times we didn't achieve it. We sabotaged ourselves.

We deserved better, so why did we self-limit? I became fascinated with this repetitive phenomenon that even the most successful people seemed to exhibit — from Richard Nixon to Jim Bakker, from Gary Hart to Michael Miliken.

This book is about what we deserve to have in life and how we can stop sabotaging getting it.

Deserve Quotient psychology can be clearly observed in the personal stories of people who are still unaware of how they do themselves in.

## THE HOUSE THAT JACK WRECKED

Jack was a great insurance salesman. He earned more commissions than anyone in his agency.

His dream was to have his own company. He loved the idea of the challenge and fun of running his own business. When his agency head decided to retire, Jack bought the agency.

Eight months later, Jack could be found staring blankly out the window, yelling at his salespeople, and generally ruining everyone's day. The daily management of an office was killing him.

He was a stellar salesperson, but he was not a manager. He loved interacting with people, hated planning and detail. When his paperwork began to backlog he became rigid, compulsive, and irritable.

The sales force, uneasy without effective management, was in mutiny. Jack kept denying the reality of reduced premium flow and declining profits, hoping his "luck" would change.

Jack lost $250,000 before admitting he was in the wrong part of the business. He still could have implemented changes that would have saved his business, but his denial prevented him from acknowledging reality. What he would not see, he could not change.

## BEAUTIFUL AND ALONE

Carol is a beautiful, bright attorney with everything going for her. She is a balanced woman with many interests and friends. She divides her time between a successful law practice, volunteer work with abused kids, and many singles groups and activities.

Extroverted and entertaining, she attracts many men and dates often. That's when her sabotage begins.

She gets in a relationship and really wants it to work. For about six months she is passionately involved with a partner. Then, like clockwork, she decides he is going to leave her.

She won't return the man's phone calls, talk with him, or discuss the problem. She simply withdraws all affection and attention.

As Carol says, "I don't want to be one of those women who just hang on long after the love is gone." What she wants is a good relationships. What she has is a long list of ex-boyfriends.

## THE RICH LITTLE POOR GIRL

Sheila had a rare gift for connecting with people. After selling hard just to get the job, she made $60,000 her first year in radio sales. She had arrived.

Her "arrival" made her very nervous. Maybe other people at the station wouldn't like the successful Sheila. That is what had happened to her in school — it seemed that every time she got an award, the other kids pulled away from her.

The second year she made $40,000.

She says, "I'd like to make more, but I feel uncomfortable being that successful."

Sheila grew up poor. The idea that she could make over $20,000 a year was hard for her to believe. Her family was initially proud of her success, but soon began to make veiled disparaging comments about her getting fancier than the rest of them.

She had success, but she threw it away. At some level Sheila believed she didn't deserve it or that she might have to pay for it. She also felt a vague disloyalty to her roots.

**THE SHY GUY**

Rick is a shy, intelligent CPA with a large accounting firm. He wants to have a good relationship but gets afraid every time he starts to meet a lady.

He says, "I've always been bashful. I just don't know what to say to the girls I meet — so I don't meet them. I stand in the corner at parties and study my feet."

I told Rick that he was sabotaging his goal of having a good relationship. He decided to take the plunge and actually meet someone at a party he'd been invited to.

The next week he came into my office feeling very self-satisfied. When I asked what had happened, he said he'd gone to the party and met someone. "I walked into this party and decided I would look over all the women there and select the one I wanted to meet. I picked her out and then I avoided her at all costs! Later, I met someone else."

Rick was making some advances in his Deserve Quotient, but he was still settling for second best.

## THE PAIN IN THE NECK

Brilliant, talented, a vice-president of a large multi-national company, Todd was a man on the rise. He did his work flawlessly, came up with innovative techniques, turned in superb performance. Todd was virtually perfect.

The president of his division respected and liked him. With the employees, however, there was an entirely different scenario. Todd drove everybody crazy with his perfectionism. He corrected everyone's slightest imperfections, pointing out ways they could improve everything from their memo-writing to their exercise programs. He constantly interrupted people and debated the smallest points.

Wherever Todd moved, behind him he left a wake of angry people.

Despite his competence, his interpersonal problems created a fatal flaw for his ambitions.

Jack, Carol, Sheila, Rick, and Todd are all bright, competent people who managed to find a way to sabotage an achievement they held dear. Their **unconscious roadblocks** prevented them from reaching or holding onto that desired outcome.

As one man ruefully said:

**I always figure out a way
to snatch defeat
from the jaws of victory.**

He is not alone. Every day of the week intelligent, motivated people do themselves in with self-sabotage, using strategies of which they may be completely oblivious at a conscious level.
The next chapter examines some of those sabotage strategies.

•2•

# Sabotage Strategies
## How not to get there from here

*"You gain strength, courage, confidence by every experience in which you really stop to look fear in the face...you must do the thing you think you cannot."*
*Eleanor Roosevelt*

Over and over again we see in the media, in our friends, and in ourselves how we human beings sabotage ourselves. Sabotages are the single most frustrating part of everyone's life. There is tantalizing anguish in "I just can't quite get there".

Sabotages are straitjackets on our behavior and our feelings, restraining us from getting what we want, even though we desperately and determinedly want it.

That seems a little perverse — why in the world would we do that? The answer is, we don't do it intentionally; it is unconscious.

We all sabotage; the question is, to what extent do we hurt ourselves? We can sabotage on large levels and on small levels.

Fear is the operative agent in sabotage.

Whatever we fear, if we fear it long enough we will make it happen.

If we fear abandonment, we will abandon first — and often we abandon ourselves as well as someone else.

If we fear rejection, we reject ourselves first. If we fear success, we make sure we don't get it. Failure is bad enough, but success might be worse.

If we fear intimacy, we pick people we can never get close to.

Whatever we fear, if we do not confront and resolve it, the fear wins.

As Gerald Jampolsky says in his book Love is Letting Go of Fear, "The world we see that seems so insane may be the result of a belief system that isn't working. The belief system holds that the fearful past will extend into a fearful future, making the past and the future one. It is our memory of fear and pain that makes us feel so vulnerable. It is this feeling of vulnerability that makes us want to control and predict the future at all costs."

The paradoxical nature of fear is that by focusing on what we fear, we raise the chances of it happening. By trying to control our lives so it won't happen, we give energy to its occurrence as a sabotage to our dreams.

In Frank Herbert's science fiction classic Dune there is a wonderful mantra-rite for dispelling fear.

"I must not fear. Fear is the mind-killer. Fear is the little-death that brings total obliteration. I will face my fear. I will permit it to pass over and through me. And when it has gone past, I will turn the inner eye to see its path. Where the fear has gone there will be nothing. Only I will remain."

The challenge for all of us is to face our fear, to be in charge of it rather than letting the fear be in charge of us. Until we face it, it will win every time — and fear remains the fuel for the vehicle that is our Sabotage.

The first step in mastering fear and raising your **Deserve Quotient** is to understand your Sabotage Strategies, the ways in which you adjust your life to stay within your self-chosen limits.

## SABOTAGE STRATEGIES

**#1** **Resignation.** "Deep down I don't believe I deserve it, so I won't even go after it." "I don't like to get my hopes up. Then, if I don't get it, it won't hurt so much."

**#2** **Throwing it away.** "I get it, and then, because I don't believe I deserve it, I blow it."

**#3** **Settling.** "I want it, but I don't believe I'm good enough, so I'll settle for less." "I won't try very hard because I probably won't get it anyway."

**#4** **Denial.** "I won't pay any attention to this problem. It will just go away."

**#5** **The Fatal Flaw.** People who use this strategy may elevate themselves by taking all the right steps but have a crucial personality problem — perfectionism, excessive drinking, hairtrigger temper, overwhelming guilt — that undoes all their best efforts.

What each of these programs has in common is an underlying sense of **not deserving** the desired goal. The crucial cornerstone of changing your unconscious sabotages is to become explicitly aware of your own internal Deserve Quotient. Once you understand that which has been outside your conscious awareness, then and only then do you have a chance to change it.

# •3•

# Understanding your deserve quotient

*"If I had the mental constitution to live inside the nutshell and think myself King of Infinite Space, that would be just fine. But that's not how I am."*
*"Every man born has to carry his life to a certain depth or else."*

*Saul Bellow, Henderson the Rain King*

## DESERVE QUOTIENT — WHAT IS IT?

Your Deserve Quotient is comprised of your conscious and unconscious beliefs about what you can and are supposed to achieve in your life.

I am using the word "quotient" in its metaphoric rather than literal sense. Just as your Intelligence Quotient is an indicator of your level of intelligence, your Deserve Quotient is a gauge of the degree to which you believe you deserve what you want in various areas of life. These Deserve Levels are self-chosen and can be changed.

Of course, you consciously believe you deserve to feel happy, financially secure, loved, free of inappropriate guilt and negativity.

Perhaps you even listen to positive thinking tapes, or tell yourself daily that every day in every way you are getting better and better. And you believe it — consciously.

You were probably taught the myth that if you were kind, obeyed orders, and used your head, you would get what you wanted out of life — a sort of award because you had earned it with your good behavior. Conversely, if bad things happened it was probably your fault — "you should have thought about that before you did it" — and you deserved what you got.

This concept of earning or controlling all the outcomes of our lives is flawed. You cannot control major acts of God, the economy, or other people's feelings. That's the bad news.

The good news is, you are in charge of your own choices, feelings, and behaviors. That is where you can make a change.

As a psychotherapist I work all day long with people who want more in their lives. I noticed that some people never seemed to get what they wanted. It was too easy for me to shrug it off and say, "Well, they didn't commit to therapy, didn't really work for it." Some of them worked really hard! But they still were not able to achieve what they wanted in their lives.

I began to ask myself, "Why?" With all their genuine motivation and application of techniques, why didn't they improve?

The answer, I believe, is that they didn't believe they deserved to get what they said they wanted.

I became very much aware of this in my own life.

I grew up in a small midwestern town in the standard 1950's and '60's way. My father was a successful national book salesman. My mother was a college professor.

I first experienced my own Deserve Quotient issues after college. Near the end of my senior year I had fallen in love with my college professor. He was young, brilliant, everything I believed I wanted in a romantic partner. I felt swept off my feet.

After graduation, he suggested that I move to Boston to be with him when he started his new job at Harvard. I instantly said yes. But before we went to Boston, he asked me to travel with his family to Europe for the summer.

I felt I had won an emotional sweepstakes. Cinderella had nothing on me! I joyfully went to Europe and Boston, ignoring my friends' and family's cautions about the man and the move. I was living in Boston, a new city for me, with no job, no friends, and a newly printed degree in Political Science. No one in Boston was particularly impressed with my undergraduate degree, so I ended up selling clothes in Harvard Square.

One night I discovered him with another woman. I was shattered. It was one of those times when the world stops, when one single experience is forever stamped in our memory and changes our entire perception of the world. I had believed we would be married and live happily ever after in Cambridge. I was wrong. My fairy tale dissolved.

After many accusations and tears, I called my parents. They sent me the money to move back home.

I went back in despair. For several weeks I sat, literally sat. I was in terrible emotional pain. I lost weight, felt nauseated, couldn't sleep — or if I did fall asleep, I had nightmares. I had no interest in friends or family.

I was deeply depressed. I walked around with my shoulders pulled almost to my ears. My neck and back were in constant spasms from muscular tension.

My family became very concerned. Here was their daughter, whom they had raised and spent thousands educating, becoming a vegetable in her room. They took me to internists, family friends, clergymen, anyone they could think of to help snap me back to normal functioning. I wouldn't be helped.

Finally they began talking surgery because my shoulders seemed frozen and would not come down. Something in me finally snapped. I said, "Wait a minute. I think every bit of this is emotional."

I remembered a man I had met through friends at college, a psychotherapist. I called him, we talked on the phone, and that phone call, which became my first therapy session, changed my life.

During the call I started to cry and talk about the dream I had lost. After the call, my shoulders came down about half an inch.

I called again the next night. This time I got angry and talked about betrayal and rage. My shoulders dropped another half an inch.

By the end of the week the tension and pain were gone from my shoulders, neck, and back. I felt saved. I knew that what happened to me in Boston was something I never wanted to happen again.

I decided the only way I could make sure it didn't happen was to learn everything I could about me and my choice of men. I returned to Dallas and entered therapy with the man who had helped me on the phone.

That is how I discovered that I had a wonderful ability to choose witty, charming men who would never make a commitment to get married. My goal became how to make them change. I fell in love with "potential" and ignored the reality that they did not want the same outcome that I did.

The more they resisted my trying to change them, the harder I tried. None of those relationships were ever changed by my attempts at psychic urban renewal. I wanted to keep the outside while gutting the inside and making them into what I wanted. I failed.

In time I came to understand that at a very fundamental level I did not think I deserved what I had been seeking.

Before you can have more in your life, you have to follow the wise maxim "Know thyself." Not just your Conscious Self, but also your Unconscious Self.

That means changing at a deep and profound level. Some of that change will come quickly and easily. Other parts of it will take longer and will not be easy. It requires a commitment to the evolutionary process that is change.

The rewards can be summed up in one sentence: You can have more in your life than you have ever had.

You are the only person who is entitled to decide what that more will be. Perhaps it is more income, more loving relationships, more sense of safety, more spiritual development, more health and energy.

You already know about the stress and pain of deeply wanting someone or something, yet feeling chronically blocked from getting it. There is such frustration in trying. The painful irony is that trying doesn't work anyway. You may know someone right now who is trying to quit drinking, lose weight, give up a destructive relationship.

The only way not to feel that anguish of frustration is to fully understand and resolve the "how" and the "why" of sabotaging behaviors.

Your final decision on what you deserve is influenced by all your beliefs and feelings, conscious and unconscious. There are specific Deserve Levels for every area of your life: love, work, friends, health. Paradoxically, it is possible to have a high Deserve Level in one area (career) and a low one in another (relationships).

You were born with the fundamental right to believe the best of yourself. This entitlement is basic to every human being. Somewhere along the way, though, we begin to doubt what we deserve.

Babies have no question about their right to be loved or held. They scream when they are hungry or wet, letting the world know of their basic needs. They feel no need to apologize or justify — they just feel it! They ask for what they want and they respond spontaneously when they don't get it.

And then something happens. It is subtle and it takes a long time, but it happens. Our innate sense of deserving to feel our feelings and express our needs starts getting lost as we mature. Instead of believing we deserve love just for "being," we lower our self-esteem and try to earn approval and love by "doing." We begin to think we must earn love, and so we give up our real feelings to meet the approved image.

A two-year-old confidently attempts almost anything. He may not make it, but he will darn well try if he isn't prevented. As we get older, we begin to limit our beliefs about our abilities. We believe the other guy can make the higher grades, get the big sale or promotion, go after the advanced degree, win the beloved. But not us.

These feelings and beliefs sabotage our confidence. They drain our psychic and physical energy. They are like a low-grade infection that is too subtle to diagnose, and the outcome is that we feel defeated before we begin. We may be willing to give it that old college try, but in our hearts we know we are just trying, not succeeding.

Change takes time. Deserving more means you will expand your beliefs, your feelings, and your spirituality — expand the limits of your Deserve Quotient. It is an inner journey, a unification, that becomes an outer reality.

This is not magic. It is a purposeful alignment of your beliefs, choices, focus and energy.

With my clients, as in my own life, I have come to learn that we don't allow ourselves to have what we want until we believe — truly believe — that we deserve it.

Specific wants differ from person to person. One wants to find a husband, another to build a fortune, another to be free from anxiety, another to make a marriage work. Regardless of the wish, there is a vast chasm between what we say we want and what we believe we deserve.

We get what we believe we deserve. No more, no less. We never exceed our own expectations, at least not for long. Our psychological comfort zones mediate our Deserve Level limits. If we achieve beyond our comfort zone, we face a choice — to increase our Deserve Level limits to encompass this increase, or to give away what we have achieved.

Our beliefs about what we deserve subtly create our reality. We live out the reality of our constraints rather than soaring with the vision of the possible.

To have a full, happy life, we have to be congruent between what we want and what we believe we deserve. The bridge between what we want and what we deserve is our personal expectations.

**NEGATIVE EXPECTATIONS = don't deserve it**
**(I'll sabotage getting it)**

**POSITIVE EXPECTATIONS = I deserve it**
**(I'll facilitate getting it)**

Before I increased my Deserve Level in relationships, I had a low-level dread and expectation that they would not work out. I wanted to find the man of my dreams but I expected that the relationship wouldn't last. This expectation was based on my lack of self-esteem, my belief system, and my personal history.

We cannot be aware of our unconscious beliefs, but we can see the evidence of them by what we have in our lives. If we can change our Deserve Level, we can begin to expect to get what we want — and we can become congruent with wanting and deserving.

This congruency can lead us to actualizing our dreams.

•4•

# Beliefs: You have to be carefully taught

"I don't believe it," said Luke Skywalker.
"That is why you fail," said Yoda.

— *The Empire Strikes Back*

This song from South Pacific sums up how we all get our belief systems. "You have to be carefully taught to hate and fear, it has to be drummed into your dear little ear. You have to be carefully taught."

All of us are carefully taught. In growing up you enroll in an eighteen-year course called LIFE BELIEFS. This course covers all areas of your life — religion, career, style, success, who to marry or not to marry, pleasure, friends, health, and so on. This course is quite complete. It's taught to us with daily lessons and homework by experienced teachers, usually our parents. The material they teach us has a lived-in feel because it was taught to them as children.

We absorb our beliefs from these people we grew up with — not always the beliefs they said they had, but always the ones they lived. Many times in therapy I hear clients say, "Oh, my God, I sound just like my mother!" They are surprised to realize they are responding in a similar way to their parents' responses. It's shocking but true.

Beliefs are the repetitive statements you make to, and often about, yourself as if they were fact.

Like all of us, you grew up in a family that instructed you in word and deed in what life was to be for you. You were schooled in beliefs and expectations for yourself that were created by others.

Whether you knew it or not, you signed an emotional contract that stated what you were entitled to — but you never saw the small print. It covered your thoughts, decisions, feelings, and values.

As you grew up, the power of this emotional covenant continued to assert itself. Your beliefs were reflected in the people you chose to love and be close to, the career you chose to establish, the amount of money you earned, and your level of physical and emotional health.

## READING THE FINE PRINT

Some of your beliefs are positive and some aren't. Maybe you were the person in your family who was supposed to be the success, or maybe you were supposed to try hard and barely make it.

Maybe you were programmed to have a wonderful, loving marriage, but can't ever get it together to have a career. Or maybe you were supposed to make it great in a career, but had no skills or example for making a relationship work.

Just because you have permission in one area doesn't mean you have it in another. You have separate beliefs in every area of your life — and your beliefs shape your view of the world.

Joan Donley, a physician friend, told me a story that is a charming example of how a belief shapes your world view. Her two-year-old son had met only his mother's female doctor friends. They went to a picnic with all the doctors from the hospital and he became very excited. He ran up to her and said, "Mommy, Mommy! Men are doctors too!" His whole belief system had shifted.

## HOW DO BELIEFS EXERCISE SO MUCH POWER IN OUR LIVES?

There are two reasons why your beliefs are so powerful.

1. **Energy follows thought.** Your energy follows what you think about. If you stay with a set of negative beliefs, your energy will follow that thought — and consequently you will create more and more negative energy.

You've had days when everything you do doesn't work. You grab your briefcase and it falls open, spilling everything. Your car won't start. You've misplaced your calendar. Everything you touch seems doomed to fail, and you can barely make it through the day.

You stagger home, just glad to be off the highways, and then you get a call from your best friends. They have had something wonderful happen and want to buy you dinner and celebrate — and suddenly you are charged with new energy.

What happened? Your thoughts changed and your energy responded.

2. **Whatever you think about expands.** What you focus on is what you get more of. If you focus on how angry you are at a friend, you are going to find yourself acting madder and madder.

Because your thoughts direct your energy, and the energy you put into your activities then creates outcome, you have a perfect system of the self-fulfilling prophecy. You get back what you believe will happen even if you consciously want it NOT to happen.

This is the basis for the concept of worry. You worry about money and everything seems to drain your resources. You worry about your health and every ache seems terminal.

On the other hand, you can be excited about a new career or relationship, and you fantasize all the positives. This belief expands and you feel wonderful.

Because of the power of your beliefs, both conscious and unconscious, to dictate your experience, you keep creating what you believe to be true. Consequently, you never exceed your own expectations.

Beliefs are icebergs. Like an iceberg, what sticks up into conscious awareness comprises only about 10 percent of your total belief system. A full 90 percent of your beliefs remain unconscious to your walking-around self, until you go looking for them.

**These unknown beliefs create your thoughts and direct your energy.**

Rob did not consciously believe that all jobs were precarious. Nonetheless, he unconsciously got the idea that his job would go away some day — so he created what he feared, by setting himself up to be fired.

Without realizing it, Rob was reliving an old family tale. His dad had frequently told him about the Depression, and how you might think you have a good job, but it can get pulled out from under you any time. The only thing you could count on was that your company would never appreciate you. Didn't the railroad let him go after twenty years?

As the story got repeated over and over, Rob created a self-fulfilling prophecy. Symbolically he abandoned his jobs before his jobs had a chance to abandon him. Because he focused his thoughts on his fear, he created what he wanted to avoid.

Our beliefs become so ingrained that our behaviors reflect them in repetitive ways.

Jeff was told by his father, "You'd lose your head if it weren't attached." Jeff still can't keep track of anything! He misplaces car keys, walks away without his purchases, and generally behaves like an absent-minded professor.

## HOW DO WE GET OUR BELIEFS?

As we grow up we internalize the feelings, actions and bodily responses of the people around us. Our beliefs are a culmination of all the experiences and messages we have received from parents, siblings, church, school, television, movies, and all the myriad messages we take in.

Beliefs become engraved on us early in our lives and, if left unchanged, direct our lives from then on. Some of our beliefs obviously come to us directly, and others are from our interpretations of what people meant.

Other people's comments largely program us. What parents or others say to us is staggering in its importance to our self-esteem and self-confidence.

Shad Helmstetter, in his book What to Say When You Talk to Yourself, gives this example of the amount of negative programming most of us have experienced.

"During the first eighteen years of our lives, if we grew up in a fairly average, reasonably positive home, we were told NO, or what we could not do, more than 148,000 times. If you were a little more fortunate you may have been told NO only 100,000 times, or 50,000 times — however many, it was considerably more negative programming than any of us needs."

Helmstetter goes on to say that behavioral research tells us that as much as 77% of what we think on a daily basis is negative and works against us.

Think about that: whatever good outcomes you are creating are coming from only 23% of your potential positive energy.

Imagine what you can accomplish when you tap into some of that wonderful unused energy!

All day long you listen to this litany in your head that you aren't consciously aware of — but you can feel its drain on your energy system.

Many of our most powerful beliefs remain unconscious. They serve as the subtle "glasses," the prescription through which we view the world. Their influence on our lives is profound and our conscious awareness of them is minimal.

Deserve Level starts here and replicates itself over and over through life experience. Deserve Level at this stage has to do with feeling a basic right to get what you want or need.

This belief of one's basic right forms in the earliest object relationship, with mother. If we had "good enough" mothering, we felt nurtured during this crucial early period. When we were hungry, wet, or needed attention, the "mothering" person in our lives was there. When we reached out for closeness or warmth, someone responded appropriately.

If a disturbance arose at this time, such as mother becoming ill, depressed, or overworked, we might have felt deprived. This deprivation becomes interpreted into a belief — a belief that says, "I don't deserve love, warmth, closeness, because I don't get it when I ask for it."

Small children cannot reason with much complexity, but you can see their beliefs in their behavior. A child whose needs are seldom met becomes increasingly quieter, until at some point he will stop trying. Why keep on asking if no one responds? What's the use?

The baby gives up, feels defeated, and resents the deprivation. Dr. T. Berry Braselton, the noted pediatrician and child behaviorist, says he can tell by the time a child is nine months old whether she has decided she will or won't make it in the world.

One basic limiting belief states: "If I have to ask for it, it is not worth getting." Paul will not ask for what he wants, unconsciously battling between the part of him that hopes Heidi will "notice" and his belief that she never will.

His corollary belief, of course, is "If she loved me, she would know. If I have to ask her, it means she doesn't care."

It is an unintentional set-up to Heidi, a no-win situation for everybody. She goes crazy trying to guess what he wants.

It gets even deeper. The second part of Paul's belief is, "If she responds after I ask her, it's only because of obligation and guilt, and I don't want her to give me anything for those reasons." Or maybe the noble version, "I don't want to impose on her if she doesn't want to do it."

A set-up? Of course. Intentional? No. Paul's belief system can only acknowledge Heidi as caring when she happens to guess right about what he wants. His belief about himself — his sense of what he deserves — is very low.

Art Linkletter told a story about a little boy who exemplified a very positive belief system. For several years Art hosted a television program called the "House Party." He invited small children to be on his show. He enjoyed their candor. The first question he asked was, "Tell me what your mother told you not to say" — and they did!

One afternoon he had on a very precocious child named Scott. He asked Scott, "How were you selected to be on my show?" Scott replied, "I'm the smartest kid in my class." Art said, "That's very good. Did your teacher tell you that?" Scott said, "No, I noticed it myself!"

**DIAGNOSTIC EXERCISE:**

Think of one thing you want, and write it down. It can be anything — a relationship, career, more money, more and better friends, more spiritual development. Focus on just this one thing for the moment.

**WHAT I WANT:** ______________________________

______________________________________________

______________________________________________

______________________________________________

______________________________________________

______________________________________________

Now write down your positive and negative beliefs about this thing you want. For example, you may want a powerful and successful career, but you tell yourself that if you have it, you cannot also have a happy and fulfilling marriage.

POSITIVE BELIEFS ABOUT GETTING WHAT I WANT:

1. ____________________________________________

2. ____________________________________________

3. ____________________________________________

4. ____________________________________________

5. ____________________________________________

**NEGATIVE BELIEFS ABOUT GETTING WHAT I WANT:**

1. ____________________

2. ____________________

3. ____________________

4. ____________________

5. ____________________

Remember: The negative beliefs you have about what you want are a predominate issue in your self-sabotage.

As you will see, they play an important part in your Self-Esteem and Self-Confidence.

In the next chapter we will examine these important components of your Deserve Level.

•5•

# Self Esteem and Self Confidence

*"To be nobody but yourself in a world that tries its best day and night to make you everyone else, is to fight the hardest battle anyone can fight and never stop fighting."*

— John Pearson

Self-esteem and self-confidence are often thought of as emotionally the same. Many of us use the words interchangeably. I believe they are very different.

To have a real sense of self-esteem, you have to believe that you're lovable. I knew from my mother that she'd love me even if I burned the house down. She had a distinct preference that I didn't do that and I never did, but I knew she'd still love me. Her loving was unconditional. She loved me for my "being," my personhood. I could, and did, spend hours in my room listening to my records and putting on Clearasil, eating Twinkies, being very unproductive, and she'd still love me. In unconditional loving there are no "have to's" or demands to do something to be loved. It isn't earned, it is given.

Our level of self-confidence is based on the knowledge that we can do something worthwhile in life. When I was younger I would get out my red wagon and sell my comic books and lemonade. My dad, who was a national sales manager for a large book company, would walk by and say, "That's my girl. You're a chip off the old block." I'd get a great deal of praise for producing. The same was true when I brought home A's on my report care. I learned that I could do some things and my self-confidence slowly grew.

I knew my mother loved me no matter what I did or didn't do. She also wanted me to excel and do well, so I felt her support in both areas and were clear that they were separate in her mind. She loved me (self-esteem) and believed in my abilities to achieve (self-confidence).

With my Dad I wasn't so sure. I knew that he'd approve of me if I got good grades or performed well (self-confidence), but I wasn't so sure that he'd love me if I didn't produce. (The truth is, he loved me all the time. I just didn't believe it until later in life.)

This developed into my adult Deserve Level. I felt loved and supported by women for myself and my achievements, but believed I had to perform for men to "earn" their love. I felt I had to "dance for Daddy" or he wouldn't love me. Of course, that never worked because you can't "earn" love. It has to be given freely.

For a number of years, until I learned that, I tried hard to earn men's love and drove them away in the process. I kept producing and doing things to get them to love me. If a man in my life needed something, I took on the burden of making that happen — a new job, more money, whatever. I felt if I did enough to prove my worth and loyalty then surely he would reward me by loving me.

It didn't work that way. After a lot of failed attempts and with the help of some good therapy, I decided to give up dancing for Daddy and men's approval. I felt really scared because I believed if I ever stopped working hard for love, I wouldn't get even the meager amount of love I was receiving. As one of my friends said, "You were always so eager to please me. On the one hand that was nice, but on the other I felt tremendous pressure to be constantly pleased. It made me tense."

He was right. I was so scared of not doing it right that my tension level was very high. I would wake up sometimes with my heart racing and feeling a little nauseated, all because I wasn't sure the man in my life really loved me. This anxiety was overwhelming. I would try and channel my anxiety into "productive" activity, i.e., doing what I thought would make him love me. I would go shopping for myself and end up buying him ties, sweaters, etc. I would plan to be with my girlfriends and then, if he called, I would cancel. I was puppy-dog eager to be helpful, loving, and approved of.

My desperation to be loved was more than apparent. Men, having a built-in radar for desperate women, would quickly move away from me.

Finally, all the disappointment and heartbreak got to be too much. I entered therapy. In that process I started working on building my self-esteem and learned to stop manipulating men to give me my own approval. Only I could do that.

I felt tremendous relief. You mean I don't have to try hard to figure out how to make him love me? You mean that's not the answer to my feelings of loneliness or despair? I began a long process of loving me first, building my self-esteem, and increasing my Deserve Level in relationships.

## SELF-ESTEEM AND SELF-CONFIDENCE IN BUSINESS

Mike is an extremely self-confident salesperson in the computer industry. He is convinced that his product is the best and all potential prospects would buy it if they just knew about it. He knows that he is in control of his sales, his income, and his professional life. He is always the top producer in his company and his income reflects it.

At the same time, Mike is not happy in his personal life. Try as he will, he has never had a relationship last longer than two years. The truth is that while his self-confidence is high, Mike's self-esteem is shaky. Because he feels unsure of himself in his relationships, he tries to do things to feel better, working harder and harder. The more he works and produces, the more his self-confidence increases. Regrettably, that doesn't change his self-esteem.

**Self-confidence is conditional acknowledgment for your performance. You are acknowledged for "doing" something well.**

**Self-esteem is unconditional acknowledgment for your own worth and lovability. You are acknowledged for "being" a good person.**

Confusion between self-esteem and self-confidence creates massive stress in our lives. Because we get them intermingled in our perception, we tend to "scratch the wrong itch," to compensate inappropriately.

For healthy self-confidence you either have to do something or have reason to believe, based on past performance, that you can. You have to make your quota, or put together a great deal, or run a five-minute mile.

For healthy self-esteem you need acknowledgment of who you are as a person, that you are loved and lovable just the way you are.

Self-confidence is fostered in a child by encouragement for being capable. The father who gives an Attaboy to his kid for sinking the baskets, the mother who teaches him how to ride his bike and praises his efforts, are helping him build his self-confidence. That pride of accomplishment and capability becomes transferable — if he knows how to rewire a lamp cord, he is likely to tackle another rewiring job with a degree of certainty.

Self-esteem comes from being told he is a terrific kid, whether he is doing something or not. It tells him about his worth as a person. It is not conditional upon his performance.

## JANE'S STORY

Self-esteem can be gained even through adversity if we are loved.

Jane Warfford, a national public speaker, talks about self-esteem in this excerpt from her motivational speech.

One rainy August afternoon two little sisters, four and seven, were driving their mother crazy, running and romping through the house. She decided to entertain them. She boiled some eggs, gave one to each child, put them in the living room on a piece of paper, and said, "Look, I want you to take some crayons, paint a face on your eggs, and make some egg dolls. When you get finished making them, we'll have a play with them and then we'll eat the characters."

As the girls were engrossed in their art work, the mother went to answer the doorbell. The four-year-old finished painting her egg in about two minutes, ran to where her mother was standing at the front door visiting with a neighbor, and said, "I want another egg." Her mother answered, "Wait just a minute."

The little girl went to the kitchen, pulled a stool up to the stove, crawled up on the stool, and pulled the pot forward to get another egg. As she put her hand in, it of course got burned, and when she jerked back and fell off the stool, she brought the pot down with her.

Half a gallon of boiling water poured over that little four-year-old body. She was burned from her neck to her knees — about three-quarters of her body. She spent seven months in the hospital, with every complication a burn victim can endure. The worst was that her teeth all rotted and fell out, and every week they came in with the razors and shaved her head.

But she lived, and that was a miracle.

Her parents were so delighted that their daughter had made it through the ordeal, they forgot to tell her what she looked like. She when it came time to go home, she was not prepared for what she would find.

The first thing she was going to do was to go Sunday School. For this little girl that meant to have fun. It had been a long time since she had had any fun. That Sunday morning she got up very early — she was so excited about finally getting to do something. It was like Christmas morning.

She went to her Sunday School class, but she didn't have fun. Nobody would have anything to do with her. The children were frightened of her, some of them laughed at her, and nobody played with her. When her mother came to pick her up, she looked down at her child and saw that the burns had healed but that the emotional scars were very deep.

She took her little girl home and put her up on the bed. And this is what that mother told that child that day.

She said, "What is beautiful about you is on the inside."

And that mother told that little girl those words every single day. She never missed one day. Sometimes the child would come in from playing and say, "Everybody hates me because I am so ugly." And the mother would say, "Oh, no, I love you. And you're beautiful. Look inside."

When she went to the first grade … e didn't look a lot better. She still didn't … teeth. Her scars were very promi… grew in funny patches. T… actually called the sch… hild can't learn if he has t… ne."

B… got her teeth, her … e, the children were … hat her life was going …

… turned nine she had an- … She became a cancer patient. … of the first children in that little … town ever to have chemotherapy, and it saved her life. She again lost her hair.

From the time she was four until she was thirteen, there are no pictures of that child — except for the one that the mother put in the little girl's mind, and that was, "You are beautiful. Look inside."

I was that child. That was my childhood.

Jane tells this story, not for pity, but for illustration. We all have scars, emotional and physical, and we need a healthy self-esteem to survive those experiences.

## ELLEN'S STORY

Ellen Terry is a charming, attractive woman in her mid-forties with two children. Fifteen years ago she was the wife of a very successful banker, living a lifestyle we would all envy. She divided her time between important charities, tennis, Junior League, and friends.

One afternoon, while she was hosting a charity tea, there was a knock on the door. She answered and was told by the man on her doorstep, "I've come to repossess your Mercedes."

Ellen first thought there had been a mistake. Her disbelief turned to dismay as she learned that no payments had been made on the car loan in months. Thus began a devastating nightmare that included financial ruin, divorce, and a seven-month separation from her two children, who went to live with their grandparents while Ellen tried to figure out what to do.

She began by liquidating all her assets in an effort to pay creditors. Her house, jewelry, most of her clothes, everything had to go. Even then, she was still left owing more than $100,000 to the IRS.

Ellen Terry had no car, no job, no apparent workplace skills. She did, however, have a legacy from childhood — a feeling of self-worth given to her by her parents. She'd been told to be a fighter, not a quitter.

She says, "My dad, who was all of 5-foot-5-inches and wore size 5 cowboy boots, always told me the only inches that mattered were the six inches between your two ears, and whether you perceived things positively or negatively. He taught me that perceiving the glass as half-full or half-empty is up to you." She pulled herself up to her full 4-foot-10-inch height and started fighting.

Her first goal was to get a job quickly, one that would make enough money for her to bring her kids back home. On her brother's advice, she decided to pursue residential real estate. Most people, she says, discouraged her, saying it was not a promising career and would take six months to a year to make a sale. Undaunted, she tenaciously interviewed real estate companies. Finally she persuaded Coldwell Banker, then the largest nationwide real estate company, to give her a chance.

She says, "I felt like the rabbit that was being chased by the fox. When the farmer yelled out, 'Hey rabbit, you gonna make it?" the rabbit hollered back, 'Make it? Man, I gotta make it!'"

The day she passed the exam she wrote her first contract. Within six weeks she had sold two houses and made $12,000. By the end of her first full year she was Coldwell Banker's top salesperson in Texas and second in the nation.

A couple of years later she opened her own company, which is known in Dallas as the "Neiman-Marcus of residential real estate." It has logged over a billion dollars in residential sales, many representing multimillion dollar homes.

Ellen Terry says, "I believe there are absolutely no restrictions on what you can do except the ones you create in your own mind. Success is a matter of being committed to excellence in whatever you do."

## HIGH SELF-ESTEEM, LOW SELF-CONFIDENCE

Look at Margaret, the 50-year-old affluent housewife who has many wonderful, loving relationships. She is at a time in her life when her children are grown, her husband has retired, and she also has retired from her mothering role. She is tired of volunteer work and she wants to do something in the marketplace, to produce. She has high self-esteem but low self-confidence, because she is thinking of entering an area that is new to her. She does not have the experience to reassure herself that she will be able to perform well.

"I'd love to go into cosmetic sales," she says, "but I'm just terrified. I don't know if I can do it. What if I fall flat on my face? I want to try, but I'm just too scared."

Her self-esteem is okay. It's her self-confidence that she needs to work on.

**HIGH SELF-CONFIDENCE, LOW SELF-ESTEEM**

Ironically, whether we lack self-confidence or self-esteem, we tend to make up the deficiency by using the skills we have in the opposite arena.

Mike the salesman, for example, used his ability to perform and produce when he tried to create good relationships. He would try to razzle-dazzle and charm his partner, trying to "make her love him." Naturally, this just didn't work. You can't "sell" anyone on loving you. You can only be yourself — and either they do or they don't.

People with high self-confidence and low self-esteem tend to be pretty structured and goal-directed. This is a good work habit, but when you bring it home, you try to control your mate and run the show. These people often have a great deal of interpersonal difficulty; the skills that work well in one area may not in the other.

To compensate, they throw themselves into their job for comfort and they overachieve. Often they make work a substitute for social life or friends.

At work they seem to have it made, but in their personal life they are so out of balance that they try to nurture themselves with destructive outlets like excessive drinking, illegal drugs, or compulsive sexual encounters.

On the other hand, the person with high self-esteem but low self-confidence might trade on his people skills to the detriment of performance. Sales managers have heard it often: "I'm a nice person, a good guy, and we're friends. Come on, keep me on board even though I never make my quota."

As a manager, you don't want to fire such people because they really are likable — but the truth is, they just can't produce.

Managers are also familiar with the person who is fabulous as a producer but is a nightmare to work with. Joyce is one of those. A top producer in commercial real estate leasing, Joyce simply can't seem to get along with any manager. She sees them all as parental figures, and she rebels. She refuses their direction, talks back, tells them they don't know what they're talking about.

Joyce refuses to let anybody have authority over her.

Joyce also keeps getting fired.

Her sales performance is superb, but she is so horrible to deal with, it's finally just not worth it to the beleagured manager or, indeed, the organization. Joyce sabotages herself because of her low self-esteem.

There are two important and different aspects operating: likability and productivity. A person who is simply likable but does not produce is bad for the company. A person who is a great producer but is hell to deal with may be good for the company in the short haul, but bad when everyone gets fed up with the prima donna tactics.

## IMPLICATIONS FOR THE MANAGER

Bernie Dorin of Unocal said in a management memo: "I have three core beliefs which I feel must constitute the basis for whatever approach I put into place.

1. Honest, open discussion can solve most problems, and in many cases avoid them before they arise.

2. Positive reinforcement of effort and competence leads to increased self-confidence. Positive acknowledgment of people leads to increased self-esteem.

3. Self-esteem and self-confidence enhance productivity, creativity, risk-taking, and personal satisfaction with work.

"These three beliefs are obviously linked, and if put into practice, serve to reinforce the mature type of relationships between supervisor and employee that should be the goal of management, rather than the parent-to-child relationships that often occurs. While acting like a parent takes much of the uncertainty out of a situation and helps the supervisor maintain a feeling of control, the development of the employee is stunted and all parties lose. Only an adult-to-adult relationship fosters the growth of both participants."

## HOW DO YOU STACK UP?

If you try to take self-esteem to the office and ask to be unconditionally regarded whether you produce or not, you are asking the impossible.

It is critical to balance your self-confidence and self-esteem. Why? Because you are a whole person. Eventually you will pay the price for being out of balance.

If you have more self-confidence than self-esteem, you may be nice and charming, but you tend to get addicted to work and try to get it to take the place of close relationships. You probably don't have a support system.

If you have more self-esteem than self-confidence, you are thoughtful, considerate, and feel good, but you may lack drive. Less achievement-oriented, you get high on having good relationships, even at work, and you may not want to concentrate on business.

## WHERE ARE YOU?

**In Self-Esteem I rate myself:**

**1 2 3 4 5 6 7 8 9 10**

**In Self-Confidence I rate myself:**

**1 2 3 4 5 6 7 8 9 10**

Whichever one gets the lower rating is the groove on the record where your needle always gets stuck. It is the one you think about when you're driving home alone after work. If your love life is terrible, you'll focus on that. If your sales are off, you'll focus on that. Whichever it is, you need to do the things that will bring you into balance.

Inside all of us is the need to finish our unfinished business, to bring the two aspects of our lives into balance.

If you lack self-confidence, start paying attention to things you do well. Get acknowledgment from others. DO the things it will take to get that increased self-confidence.

If you lack self-esteem, give yourself time to **be** with people and share feelings, get to know them, and put aside work-oriented activity as the only way of life. Focus on liking, loving, and feeling. Those are the reasons we are alive.

How you live your life is up to you. If you balance your self-esteem and self-confidence, you will find that they comprise a healthy sense of self-worth. If you do what it takes to bring your life into balance, you will have few regrets, because your business and personal life will bring you the rewards you seek — a high Deserve Level and an enhanced passion for being alive.

# •6•

# Permission from your past

"The past is prologue."

*— inscription on the treasury Building, Washington, D.C.*

All of us grew up in families that gave us or withheld permission for success. Some of us had families that cheered us on at whatever we wanted to achieve. Others came from families that were more cautious, a little scared for us, and their admonitions held us back.

Within this culture there are specific roles that men and women get told they can do. If you wanted to do something that was out of that role, you may not have received permission to do it. Then you had to struggle with giving yourself permission.

Your programs for living — what you heard about yourself, or what your parents did with their lives, the models they showed you — are part of your permission system.

You inherited your permissions from all the stories, myths, and statements that your family or important mentors, made about you. You were told about your abilities, in word and behavior, by the people closest to you. Your personal beliefs about yourself are scripted into your permissions system. These permissions follow you and direct your life's course.

Maybe you are a "people person," an extrovert just like Dad. Dad happens to be a top-ranked insurance salesman, so naturally you'd be good in sales.

Sometimes your permissions come from important people other than your parents. Jim's leadership abilities were anchored into his unconscious by a strong relationship with his parish priest.

Jim was trained in life lessons by the Jesuits' beliefs in service and sacrifice for others. He became the youth fellowship president of his church club. One afternoon his mentor came up to him, took hold of his arm, and said, "You will be a very important man one day. You are a leader of men."

This permission went right through to Jim's unconscious and became a powerful psychological imprint. He grew up to become a recognized leader in the broadcasting field and a highly active community leader. His internal permissions led him to serve others while expecting less for himself.

Some of us have a **lack of permission** from our past. When we start to go after something, we run into blocks and sabotage ourselves because inside ourselves we don't believe it is possible. This can create enormous conflict within us.

Phyllis wants to have a successful career and also be a loving, effective wife and mother. When she was growing up she saw women who did one or the other, but no-one who did both successfully. Her mother never believed that she could have both. Phyllis has to create new permission, based on role models she sees now, women who do manage to balance several roles and still take care of themselves.

Maybe you got **mixed permission**. From one parent you may have heard, "You can't do that!" and from the other "That's great, kid, you can do it!" When you start to move toward a new goal that pushes you beyond your comfort zone, you get two messages in your head. Guess what? Your action becomes ambivalent, one step forward and one step back, depending upon which permission is more active at that moment.

A lot of people got mixed permission from the same parent. One time we'd hear one thing, and another time another. It takes some sorting to figure out what you have been paying most attention to.

Sometimes a parent says one thing and acts another, which means you may have learned to do the same thing. The classic line is, "Do what I say, not what I do."

Your parents did the best job they could and loved you the very best way they knew how. Sometimes what you heard was not what they said, but rather how you interpreted it out of your own perception.

Your parents may now have tremendous support for you without your realizing it. The limitations they placed on you when you were small may have long since disappeared in their minds but not in yours.

A lot of people live out the permission they had at age five, and if they do not update, they will stay the same.

If you believed you were shy, retiring, and could not have good relationships back then, unless you change that early program you might live it out your whole life.

Sally had spent thousands of dollars on therapy and still could not seem to make a relationship work. She did an exercise in my seminar in which she closed her eyes and told her mother what she wanted (which was a fifth husband), then clearly heard her mother say, "Don't fool with them, they'll all leave you anyway." No wonder none of her relationships ever lasted.

The challenge is for you to give yourself new permission to let yourself believe you can have what you want. You can find other sources, within yourself and from other people, to get the permission you do not currently have.

Changing permission can have powerful outcomes. Sue was making about thirty thousand dollars a year in real estate sales commissions and was frustrated because she could not seem to make more. In discussing her Deserve Level with me, she discovered that her father had never made more than thirty thousand dollars a year — and she believed that if she did better than her father, he would not love her any more. Her mother had died, her marriage had ended, and her dad's love was much more important to her than the additional money.

Every time she started to make more, she got sick, got fired, or found some other way to sabotage herself.

When she began the process of increasing her Deserve Level, she contacted her father in west Texas and asked him pointblank how he felt about the money issue. His reply was, "Why, darlin', you make all the money you can and want to! I'll come to Dallas and let you buy me a steak dinner."

A few months later she got into computer sales. Her first commission was $15,000, half of what she had formerly made in six months. Her annual earnings that year were $150,000! She did so well that she broke every sales record in her company — by getting out of her own way. She found out where her permission stopped, where the conflict was, and resolved that conflict. I told her that if I'd had a higher Deserve Level, I'd have charged her a commission, not a flat fee!

Few people will find it productive to actually go back to their parents and try to get the permission they did not get thirty years ago. You will know by your behavior what you got and did not get. There is no magic in this: just look at your outcomes, at what you are doing, and from them you will be able to trace back to the origins.

Once you know what it is that your internal permission system has not been allowing you to have, you can change it. Until then, you are stuck into blaming outside factors.

We look for excuses, we pass the buck, if we will not take responsibility for how we are blocked:

"The economy is lousy."
"There are no good single men/women left."
"It was office politics."
"They discriminate against people like me."
"I was so good I intimidated them."

You have the power not only to find out how you are blocked, but also the power to change it. That is a lot better, isn't it, than thinking that "life is doing it" to you — because from that position you do not have any power.

**DIAGNOSTIC EXERCISE:**

Think of something you want for yourself. It can be anything — more money, better love life, a new car, anything.

Now fantasize that you're talking with your father and you tell him what you want for yourself. What is his response? How does he look? What is he saying? Is he supportive, disbelieving or critical?

Now pretend you are talking with your mother. What is her response? Look at her face. Is she with you or not? What does she say about your wants?

Review your parents' different responses. Who do you feel supported by? Do you have permission to get what you want?

What are the messages you got from your parents? You may still treat yourself the same way you were treated. If you didn't like any of the responses you got, check to be sure that you are not still giving yourself these same messages.

Give yourself a few minutes to think about all this. Jot down what permissions you do or do not have, and star the ones you want to have more of.

Now that you understand the unconscious power of **permission from your past**, you are ready to move into a powerful new phase: deciding what you really want. Not what others wanted for you, not what you are "supposed" to want, but what <u>you</u> really want.

•7•

# Discovering what you want: Name it to caim it

"If man advances confidently in the direction of his dreams and endeavors to lead the life which he has imagined, he will meet with a success unexpected in common hours."

*Henry David Thoreau*

As with any journey, before you can map your route you have to know where you are starting.

**IDENTIFYING YOUR DESERVE LEVEL**

Quickly and spontaneously, circle your answers to these questions:

Next year, I believe I will make:

1) $10,000------15,000
2) 15,000------30,000
3) 30,000------45,000
4) 45,000------60,000
5) 60,000------75,000
6) 75,000 ----100,000
7) 100,000 ----125,000
8) 125,000 ----150,000
9) 150,000 ----200,000
10) 200,000 ---250,000
11) more than $250,000

I believe I can have the material things I want.

1) Never
2) Almost never
3) Sometimes
4) Most of the time
5) Always

I believe I can have a good, loving relationship.

1) Never
2) Almost never
3) Sometimes
4) Most of the time
5) Always

I feel lovable and capable of loving others.

1) Never
2) Almost never
3) Sometimes
4) Most of the time
5) Always

I feel I can produce and perform well at my job or career.

1) Never
2) Almost never
3) Sometimes
4) Most of the time
5) Always

I would rate my love life:

1) Very low satisfaction
2) Medium low satisfaction
3) Medium satisfaction
4) Medium high satisfaction
5) High satisfaction

I would rate my work life (income, work climate, liking of my job):

1) Very low satisfaction
2) Medium low satisfaction
3) Medium satisfaction
4) Medium high satisfaction
5) High satisfaction

I would rate my social contacts and friends:

1) Very low satisfaction
2) Medium low satisfaction
3) Medium satisfaction
4) Medium high satisfaction
5) High satisfaction

I feel capable of getting what I desire from life:

1) Never
2) Almost never
3) Sometimes
4) Most of the time
5) Always

My parents believe I'm a worthwhile, competent, and lovable person:

1) Never
2) Almost never
3) Sometimes
4) Most of the time
5) Always

**SCORING**

Add up the numbers of the answers you circled.

**Below 20 points - Low Deserve Level**

You don't truly believe you can have much in your life. Take a serious look at changing your thoughts and the statements you make to yourself about who you are and what life holds. You may want to get some counseling — your beliefs about yourself are stopping you from prosperity.

**21 - 30 points - Moderate Deserve Level**

You believe you deserve some of life's rewards, though you block the full attainment of these good feelings and events. Some directed imagery and more positive visualization of the desired outcomes would certainly move you forward.

**32 - 43 points - Higher Deserve Level**

You are more consistently in line with your positive beliefs of yourself and the world. Keep up the good work. Any hesitations or dips in self-esteem or self-confidence should be treated immediately to insure continued improvement. You're on the way!

**44 or higher - Very High Deserve Level**

You are being/doing everything right. You probably are enjoying a great many benefits from your participation in life. No doubt you are a pleasure to know and associate with, both personally and professionally.

Now you know where you currently are in your overall Deserve Level. The next step to increasing your Deserve Level is to answer this very hard question: "What do I want?"

The next step is to identify where you want to go and what is stopping you from getting there.

## THE WANTS TRACKDOWN

This exercise requires that you ask a friend to be your partner, Player A. You are Player B. Later you can reverse roles.

### PHASE 1: Awareness

Sit facing each other. Player A looks at Player B and asks: 'WHAT DO YOU WANT?" and B answers whatever comes to mind. A acts as Scribe for B and writes down the answer, then A agains asks, "WHAT DO YOU WANT?" and B gives another answer. Write-down, and again: "WHAT DO YOU WANT?"

Do not get sidetracked with comments, agreements, or chat — just repeat the exercise over and over for at least five minutes.

## WHAT DO YOU WANT?

When you have responded many times, you may be surprised by some of your answers. You may reach a level of wanting that you have not been aware of.

**PHASE 2: Sabotage Strategies**

Same procedure as before, but this time the repeated question is, "HOW ARE YOU SABOTAGING GETTING WHAT YOU WANT?" Answer this question for every want you listed.

**HOW ARE YOU SABOTAGING GETTING WHAT YOU WANT?**

If you find it difficult to answer the following question, don't be concerned. You may not yet know the "why" of your sabotage, but as you continue in this process of Sabotage Awareness, the answers will come. As you focus on asking the right question, your Unconscious will release the information. Your denial system will continue to keep you from knowing until you are ready.

## PHASE 3: WHY ARE YOU SABOTAGING? WHAT DO YOU FEAR?

Now that you have taken a reading on where you are, where you want to go, and how you have been stopping yourself, you are ready for the process by which you can **cure the sabotage and raise your deserve level.**

The four-step process is comprised of

**I.** **Self-Talk**
**II.** **Self-Release**
**III.** **Self-Nurturing**
**IV.** **Self-Support**

# •8•

# Self-Talk

"Each man (woman) holds between his hands
a silence that he wants to fulfill, so he fills it with his dreams."

"If you can't commit to something big, commit to something small."

*Merle Shain, When Lovers Are Friends*

Self-Talk is what you say in your own mind about yourself and the world.

There is a chatterer in your head that talks to you, day in and day out, about what you can do and have and be. These messages can be helpful or can greatly inhibit what happens to you. You are creating your own reality by the tape you play to yourself.

Here is the problem: most Self-Talk is at an unconscious level. The very programs that are running you are often out of your conscious awareness.

It is hard to understand the unconscious mind because no scientific data exists as to its existence and location. We only know it exists by its influence on our lives.

In any major conflict between the conscious and unconscious minds, the unconscious triumphs.

Basic feelings and needs reside in the unconscious. Our early life decisions and beliefs shape our choices and destiny.

The unconscious mind cannot make a distinction between fantasy and fact. If a person repeats over and over, "I'm shy," "I can't make cold calls," "I'm not pretty," the unconscious mind accepts it as reality, no matter what the objective truth is.

We constantly listen to this dialogue, and through its repetition we create our reality.

**AFFIRMATIONS**

Everybody has had the experience of energy following thought. Remember the last time you woke up in a bad mood and told yourself it was going to be a rotten day? Proved yourself right, didn't you?

Our Self-Talk is made up of affirmations. Affirmations are statements we make about our behavior, feelings, and self-worth, both to ourselves and others — statements so repetitive that we don't even notice them.

Some people mistakenly believe that affirmations are only positive statements. In reality, affirmations can be either negative or positive. Statements such as, "I'm always late" or "I'm a good financial planner" or "Attractive women never like me" are all affirmations.

If sabotaging self-talk is what you have been affirming to yourself, you've been creating a negative outcome. Now is the time to compose messages you would rather affirm in your own mind, both conscious and unconscious.

By using the powerful tool that is **purposeful self-talk,** you can turn unconscious limitations into a new vision of reality.

## VISUALIZATION

Visualization is a technique that uses vivid mental images as a way of improving performance and influencing outcome.

To make your affirmation even more powerful, allow yourself to visualize the desired outcome as you write or listen to the affirmation. Cut out a magazine illustration, or take a photograph, depicting the things you want.

Whether it is a boat, an elegant home or gorgeous car, a happy relationship, or a serene countenance, concentrating on an image will help to reinforce the words.

Put the picture on your bathroom mirror or your refrigerator or your dashboard. Every time you look at it you will be reminding yourself that this is what you want.

To be effective, affirmations and visualization need to be combined with action towards the goal. You can't just passively visualize a desired outcome while doing nothing toward it, and hope to achieve the results you want. Effective visualization needs to be combined with specific skills and active involvement.

The pictures we make in our minds can either help us get what we want or undermine our attempts. Joe wanted to meet attractive women. He faithfully did affirmations about being with and enjoying an attractive companion, but nothing was happening. When asked about his accompanying visualizations, he answered, "I can't really see anything about her except that she is bored and doesn't want to be with me. Then I see myself standing alone and feeling miserable." His negative pictures were sabotaging his positive affirmations.

After he began visualizing a woman turning toward him with delight on her face, his whole attitude about himself with women changed. Since the real issue is to find yourself first and then relationships will follow, it is not surprising that he made a connection with a lovely woman just a few weeks later.

Get clear on the things you want and it is amazing how they then show up. Again, it is not magic. It is a change in perception and in what kind of nonverbal messages you send out to others.

Peter Thomas and his success exemplify the visualization/affirmation process. Peter is Chairman of the Board and CEO of Century 21 of Canada. He started the company and now has six thousand employees.

Peter is a firm believer in the power of your own beliefs to create your reality. He carries with him, in his daily organizer, pictures of what he wants. When he opens a page you can see his 65-foot yacht, his airplane, and his new Rolls-Royce.

All of his "toys" he has acquired by affirming, visualizing, and organizing his life to meet his chosen goals.

Affirmation and visualization techniques have become commonplace in the world of athletics, medicine and sales.

The U.S. Olympics sports psychology experts have been using VMBR (visuo-motor-behavior rehearsal) since the early '70's. From experience we know that practice can improve performance. What athletes have learned is that some of that needed practice can go on in our minds.

VMBR involves fifteen to twenty minutes of relaxation followed by mental rehearsal in which you see yourself doing your desired behavior as well as you can do it. You see yourself jumping the moguls perfectly, or running the fastest mile even in wet weather, or bobsledding down the hill in the best time.

For challenge and variety you can change the scenes or the difficulty. What is important is the mental practice and repetitive experience of success.

Studies have shown that the athletes who use VMBR do improve their performances.

Similar visualization techniques are being used in the medical field. At the Cancer Counseling and Research Center started by Carl and Stephanie Simonton, therapists train cancer patients to visualize their cancer as loose, unorganized cells, and their immune system as healthy, powerful cells doing battle with and defeating the cancer cells. The process is repeated three times a day for twenty minutes at a time, with attention to concrete visualization of the powerful white cells.

This psychological therapy does not replace conventional medical interventions, but rather augments them.

The procedure, innovative when it was introduced eighteen years ago, is now widely replicated.

There have been remissions in predicted terminal cases, and in every case the patient has gained a sense of involvement, so that he is not just a "case" to the medical profession, but is himself part of the treatment. One of the most devastating aspects of cancer is the helplessness the patient often feels. By becoming involved in the treatment, patients feel a renewed sense of power to influence the outcome of their illness.

Many practitioners in the visualization field have found that the best results come from the most detailed and specific images. Sarah, a cancer patient with an interest in the Renaissance, saw her cancer as barbarians attacking her castle and her white blood cells as valiant white knights fighting for the holy cause. Her cancer went into remission and has remained there for three years.

In the very different field of sales training, I use visualization techniques to help promote salespeople's self-motivation. I have them place pictures of what they want on their desks: the new car, trimmer body, new house, and so on. Every time they make a sales call or pick up the phone, their visual goal is in front of them.

Another helpful technique is to write out your sales goal for the month and post it on your desk. Every time you are working or talking with a client, you are sub-vocalizing your goal.

Another visualization/affirmation tool that is beneficial for sales professionals is what I call "pre-game." . My idea for this technique came from the movie Big, with Tom Hanks. As the creative director of a toy company, he is preparing for the big meeting in his office. He's standing there holding a bunch of pencils in his hand and throwing them into the ceiling. His secretary interrupts and he says, "Don't disturb me, I'm in pre-game."

Pre-game is where we visualize the outcome we want before we go through the process. We see the new customer relationship going well before we even meet the prospect. It's taking five minutes before the sales call to predict a positive outcome.

Using these behavioral-rehearsal strategies, just close your eyes and run the movie of what you want to happen.

Sondra Ray, in her book I Deserve Love, makes excellent suggestions for writing affirmations. She suggests that you:

- Be specific and vivid in descriptions.
- See them happen.
- Write them in positive language.
- Write ten to twenty times a day
- Write them daily for three weeks.

When writing, use the first person present tense, as if what you want is happening right now.

**AFFIRMATIONS EXERCISE:**

Think about one thing you want, and write it down in the first person, present tense.

"I am now *

* "...making a hundred thousand dollars a year."

* "...enjoying a relationship with a loving, charming person who appreciates me."

* "...healthy, physically fit, and more alive."

* "...more deeply religious, spiritually developed, happy in my life."

You need to write or say your affirmation twenty times a day for twenty-one days to implant that information into your brain. It takes that many repetitions and that much frequency to implant your new belief. Remember, your old negative programs have been getting reinforced daily for decades — it only makes sense to give your mind a concentrated dose of the new message.

There are several forms your affirmation can take. You can **write** the statement twenty times every day. If you prefer, you can make a tape of yourself saying the affirmation twenty times, and then **listen** to it as you get dressed in the morning or as you drive to and from work. (Some people find it more effective to have someone else's voice saying the affirmation, utilizing the "authority effect.")

The important thing is consistency. It will not work if you write/hear the affirmation a few times today and then not again till next month.

If you hear a negative statement in response to your affirmation, ignore it and return with more force to the positive statement. If the negative reply persists, use it as a clue to discover further negative self-talk that is persisting deeper in your unconscious mind.

The brain has four states of consciousness:

- **BETA** Wide awake, alert consciousness
- **ALPHA** Relaxed and creative state
- **THETA** Where we usually fall asleep
- **DELTA** Deep sleep

We go through these four states daily. To use affirmations and visualizations to best advantage, we need to program them in at both the Beta and Alpha states. For best results, say/hear/see your affirmations when you are in Beta (energetic and wide awake) and again in Alpha (relaxed, creative, intuitive).

Accessing your Alpha state needs to occur in a protected environment. You are changing to a "twilight" state of consciousness. Obviously, you should not be driving, and you should be free from the likelihood of interruptions.

You can create an Alpha Access Tape that will help you reach the desired level of relaxation that creates optimum suggestability.

## ALPHA ACCESS TAPE

This is a self-hypnosis technique that you can use to help enter your affirmations into your most receptive mental state. To make this tape you will need only a recorder, pencil, and paper.

First write down your affirmations, exactly as you want them to be experienced. Now either get a friend to tape the following transcript, reading in a calm deliberate voice, or you do it if you want your own voice to be the one you hear.

Get very comfortable — stretch out, keep your feet straight. I want you to pretend that you're on a beach and you're sitting there in the sun. It is a very pleasant beach. It's not too hot. The sun is warm and you're looking at the water. The water is blue and crystal clear, easily washing up to the shore. As you are looking at the water, you are breathing very deeply. As the water comes up to the shore, you are inhaling, watching the water toward you. As the water goes back out to sea, you're exhaling. Watch the waves and enjoy this kind of circular process. Feel yourself inhale while the waves come up to the shore, and feel yourself exhale as the waves go back to sea.

Every time you inhale, you are taking in positive energy, oxygen, and when you exhale you are letting go of any tension that you are carrying in your body.

So easily inhale and exhale.

Starting at your feet, release the tension from your body. Focus on your toes. Breathe positive energy into your feet, and exhale out. Continue exhaling stress and negativeness until your feet are completely relaxed. Now move up to your calves. Breathe in deeply, breathing in the positives and exhaling any negative energy. Move up to your knees. Breathe in positive energy, exhale negative energy. Move up to your thighs, and once again breathe in positive energy and exhalc any negative tension.

Now, moving up to your abdomen, breathe in positive energy, breathing out any stress or tension. Move on up to your stomach. Breathe in very deeply — positive energy — breathe out any negative. Move to your chest. Breathe in positive energy, breathe out all the negatives. Let them go.

Upper arms, breathe in positive energy, breathe out any negative. Down to lower arms, hands — breathe in very deeply, positive energy, breathe out negative. Now move up to your neck, the back of your neck, breathe in positive energy, breathe out any negative energy. And to your face and the top of your head. Again breathe in the positive, breathe out the negative.

You feel very comfortable and relaxed, very unstressed. I want you to take a short journey with me. We're going to get on an elevator at the 10th floor; we are going down to the 1st floor. When the doors open at the 1st floor, we are going to walk into one of your favorite rooms. It can be a room where you already live, or this can be a room that you just think about and fantasize. But it has to be some place that feels especially good and restful to you.

Walk into the elevator and look up and see the floor that says 10. You are watching the floors as you descend, 9, and 8. You are feeling more and more relaxed. 7, 6, 5. You are feeling more and more comfortable and relaxed. 4, 3, 2. More and more relaxed. And now you are at the 1st floor. The doors open. You walk into your favorite room. This is the most comfortable and pleasant place you can imagine.

Look around this room. I want you to select a chair or a couch and sit down on it. See the couch. Feel yourself sitting down. Look at the walls. What is on the wall? Just enjoy that room in your imagination.

As you sit there, listen to your affirmations. As you listen, I am going to read them to you. Allow yourself to believe you can have them. Open up your Deserve Level and allow yourself to receive.

You are feeling relaxed, comfortable, happy with the thought of getting more of what you deserve.

Now I want you to get up from your chair and walk back to the elevator. See yourself get on the elevator at the ground floor and go slowly up to the tenth floor. First floor, 2, 3, you are feeling relaxed, happy, 4, 5, 6, feeling more alert and confident, 7, 8, 9, feeling positive and alert. And the tenth floor. The doors open and your eyes open and you are back in this room, awake and alert.

Play this tape whenever you want to focus on your goals. Do it at least once a day for three weeks, so your unconscious can absorb the material.

The outcome of affirmations can be attested to by people who committed to using them. There was a married couple, John and Marsha, who had become so irritated with each other that they were contemplating divorce. Marsha decided to affirm:

"John and I are getting along great. We love each other, have kind and positive communication, and enjoy great sex."

Every morning Marsha would play this tape while she was putting on her makeup. John thought the whole thing was mumbo-jumbo, but every morning while he was shaving at the next sink, he was listening to her affirmation.

A few weeks later Marsha said to their marriage counselor, "I don't know what's happened, but John and I are treating each other nicely." John still thought the process was hocus-pocus, but he said thoughtfully, "I guess hearing that every morning and thinking it might be possible IS influencing me."

Right now you can probably sing radio and TV jingles from the '60's or '50's or '40's. You hear certain melodies and you can sing verbatim the words that accompanied them. Unconsciously we absorbed that material until it became part of us, and then we repeated it back to ourselves to complete the loop.

Affirmations and visualization allow you to CHOOSE to take in what is in your own best interest.

**BETA ACCESS TIPS (wide-awake state)**

1. Find a reasonably contemplative time to write/hear your affirmations. Dressing, driving, unwinding after your day — these

are good times. It is unwise to listen while you are doing some strenuous task. Choose a time when you are calm and quiet and have at least ten minutes to devote to it.

2. Focus your energy and concentration into saying your affirmations the entire twenty repetitions each time, rather than five in the morning, five more at lunch, and so on.

3. The more often you say/listen to the twenty repetitions, the faster the information will be absorbed. Twice a day is better than once a day, but once a day is often enough to accomplish the desired outcome.

4. Figure out how you would sabotage the reaching of your goal, and then structure the affirmation so that it cures the sabotage message in advance. If you want to quit smoking but fear that you will gain weight, say something like "I am an elegant, slim non-smoker."

5. Use a positive statement rather than a negative one. Say, "I am an elegant, slim non-smoker" rather than "I am repulsed by the nastiness of cigarettes. I hate that I have such a vile habit."

6. Concentrate on one affirmation at a time. If you have a long list, work on just one or two at a time. Taking on more than you can reasonably handle might be a way you have sabotaged yourself in the past.

7. Recycling: as you get each thing you want, you can create a new affirmation about something else you want.

The more sensory channels you use, the better. Some people like to set their affirmations to music — they can sing them, chant them, listen to them, even dance to them. A writer/therapist friend composed this one for herself:

*(to the tune of "It's Not So Surprising")*

I do love feelin' gorgeous,
I do love lookin' gorgeous,
I just love findin' Me inside ....
I do love lookin' sexy
I do love bein' sexy,
I just love all this sexy pride.
This is my celebration,
Of my fine new relation
With this slim, healthy sexy Me.
I just love my little waist,
Derriere that's firm in place.

This is how I want to be!

I've taught affirmations/visualizations seminars around the world for the last five years. Every time I conduct a seminar for a group, I ask them to let me know when they reach their goals. I have had many happy phone calls and letters attesting to the fact that affirmations work if you just do them.

This is a small sampling of the "good news" letters I have received.

On an unusual-looking postcard from Malaysia:

*Dear Pat - I met you at a Century 21 convention in 1989. I promised to send you a card if I was able to make my trip. Well, here I am in Kota Kinabalu, Malaysia, Borneo. This has been great, worth selling houses for this experience.*

*Elaine High*
*Century 21 Pleasant Valley Properties*
*Amarillo, California*

Susan, a highly successful businesswoman in her mid-thirties, had a particularly interesting sabotage. Having fun was a high priority to her, and she was only attracted to men who could be very entertaining. The problem was they were all under-achievers or unsuccessful in their business lives, and she ended up being their financial supporters — which eventually wasn't much fun!

She had an unconscious belief that a man could not be successful in business and be fun (although she was). She went to parties and ended up liking the waiters and ignoring all her business associates.

She decided to do an affirmation that said, "I am with a fun, successful man who is a good communicator." Within six weeks Steve showed up, handsome, fun, and very successful.

Vicki Knight, General Sales Manager of KPLX-KLIF radio, Dallas, Texas: Vickie's affirmation was, "I'm experiencing a loving and supportive relationship with a wonderful and understanding man — who loves to dance!"

Vicki was re-entering the single scene after a traumatic divorce and feeling all the normal apprehensions of that process.

In her words, "I began to write my affirmations after hearing a seminar Pat put on at the Radio Advertising Bureau in February. I wrote my affirmation in my appointment book and read it or wrote it every day.

I went home for vacation in July and met Dan Swain. We went dancing and have been dancing together ever since!" Vicki and Dan were married several months after their first dance.

How about a career dream being visualized and created? Both Marie Kordus (KPWR in Los Angeles) and Marsha Reagan (KKNW in Seattle) were interested in advancing to general sales manager of their respective radio stations. They affirmed and intently focused on their goals, and within months they had the job they had wished for.

This is the letter I received from Todd Reynolds of KLOL-FM in Houston:

"Late in 1989 you spoke to KLOL sales staff and asked us to write down our goals for 1990. My goals were:

1) I am making $90,000 in 1990. I made $93,000 plus.

2) I am selling Pennzoil for 20 weeks in 1990. I sold 15 weeks which was the maximum on the buy, and I was the lead station on the buy.

3) I am selling $100,000 a month in 1990. I had two $100,000-plus months — $114,00 and $130,000, a first but not my last.

4) I am selling six new accounts a month. In 1990 I was the #1 new business biller, with a 28% improvement over all.

Thank you, Pat. It really worked, I am living proof. Self-talk is important, but positive self-talk is the key to my success. New goals for 1991 will be higher and I believe, no, I know, I will achieve them. I look forward to 1992 so I can look back on my success of '91."

John Maguire, the general sales manager of WRKO Red Sox Radio in Boston, uses affirmations as a management tool with his sales force. His account executives write performance goals (dollar amounts) and number of prospects to contact per week. When they reach these goals they are rewarded with bonuses and prizes.

To help them focus, he has them state their goals in the form of sentence-completion affirmations. Here are the 1991 affirmations of Bill Ebben, one of Red Sox Radio's top producers:

**I am billing** on September 1st, 1991, one million dollars for Atlantic Radio and Red Sox Radio.

**I am making** $90,000 in 1991. I am going to make $120,000 in 1992, earn it.

**I am living** by June 1st, 1992, in a brand new house. We will be living in a home of our own. Why? Because we are not renewing our lease — we have affirmed it.

**I am** the youngest, brightest radio AE in Boston. I am a senior account executive in the Red Sox sales office. In another year I will have learned enough to be a manager in Atlantic Radio or in another sports sales office around the country. I will no longer be a prospect. I have stepped up to the next level. I am the top biller. I have done it by January 1, 1992.

As is true with all the account executives, Bill has signed (with John) a Commitment Agreement which reads:

I hereby commit that I will give my best possible effort to achieve my goals. I am accountable to deliver daily the enthusiasm, the activity and the performance necessary to reach my goals in a timely professional manner. I am accountable to myself to do what it takes to be RED SOX radio's top biller!

Red Sox Radio and John's success have been extraordinary. Midway in the 1990 season they were billing $3.8 million. Going into the 1991 season, February 1st, their billings are at $5.6 million with two months remaining to sell.

Bill Ebben is billing $850,000 after six months in radio. At the rate he is going, he will earn

$95,000 in his first full year. The year before he earned $23,000.

Joan is a successful lawyer, an engaging woman who was frustrated in her marriage. Most of her frustration was sexual; she just wasn't excited by her husband of ten years. As she said, "I know something must be wrong with me. He's a great person, sweet and loving. I'm just not interested any more. I want to be fixed!"

We worked together for several months on how to enliven her marriage. Nothing worked.

In one session I said to her, "What do you want?" She paused a moment and said, "You want me to tell you the secret want I have?" I said yes. She responded, "I want to live in the mountains and write, but I can't do it."

I said, "Why can't you?" She said, "I have a practice, my husband, and my hot tub. I can't give up all that to go and live simply in the mountains."

We ended the session but I was bothered. No wonder therapy wasn't working. She didn't want it to, although she consciously wouldn't have said that.

We worked for another six weeks when she decided to give herself a month off for self-reflection. During that month she went to the mountains and gave her dream a trial run. She began to actively write her affirmation and visualize herself doing it.

Four months later she was divorced and had moved to the mountains and begun to live her secret dream. In a letter to me she says,

"I don't miss my old job. That's been a slight surprise. I've gotten a wonderful perspective on what I used to do for a living, just being away from it. I've turned into a human being instead of a robot.

I wake early each day, in time to see the sun coming over the mountains. I walk a lot, listening to the river, give the rare mountain air its depth, and spend evenings enjoying the darkness unimagined by those who have never seen a sky devoid of reflected city lights.

I write incessantly. I hear your little voice in my head often, but now I'm also hearing my little voice in my heart. And it sounds wonderful."

She got what she wanted once she allowed herself to know what it was. She lived her dream.

All the people in these stories had attended my seminar and heard me ask them to let me know when they reached their goals. I told them that if they'd let me know, I would take them with me when I reached my goal, which is to be on Oprah Winfrey's show talking about this book!

In my work I have found that most people take more time balancing their checkbooks or planning their grocery lists than they do in writing down what they want for a relationship, career or health goal. We make lists for everything from laundry to Christmas presents, yet we don't make a list of what we want in our lives.

You had little or no control over the programming of your earlier life that brought you to this stage, but you can take control of the rest of your life if you choose. To paraphrase Thornton Wilder in The Bridge of San Luis Rey,

> "We either live and die by chance, or we live and die by a plan."

You can choose. Through repetition of affirmations and visualizations, you can reprogram yourself to a more abundant life, however you define it.

# •9•

# Self-Release: Telling yourself the Truth About your Feelings

"When you become lonely and you become afraid, all the answers you will ever need will be found within yourself. Do not look so frantically out into the world for the answers to your questions. Look within and ask yourself, 'Am I being faithful to my own truth?' Losing that faith is the only real sin."

*Lynn Andrews, The Woman of Wyrrd*

Every self-help book agrees positive Self-Talk is necessary, but why isn't it enough? Why doesn't everybody who reads a positive-thinking book get what he wants?

To answer that question, look again at SELF-CONFIDENCE and SELF-ESTEEM. Each is necessary but not sufficient.

The same is true of THOUGHTS and FEELINGS. Changing Self-Talk from negative to positive is a process based on chosen thoughts. The other part that can keep us stuck, no matter how fervently we follow a self-help program, is our unresolved feelings. In the process of increasing your Deserve Level, you need to get your feelings as clear and authentic as you can. When you have learned to integrate your thoughts and your feelings so they are congruent, honoring both, you have complete permission to have what you want. Most of us do not like to acknowledge our "negative" feelings. We would like it if they were gone — if we never felt mad or sad or frustrated or hurt or upset again. We would like those painful feelings just to go away, but that is not how the mind works.

You have to express your feelings to be able to release them and get free of their negative impact. Then, and only then, can positive Self-Talk find a place to get in and stay in. Otherwise, your negative feelings will do a seek-and-destroy mission on your positive Self-Talk.

There are two important premises about feelings:

1) Feelings are "facts."
2) There are only two ways feelings can be expressed — out (released) or in (contained.)

**FEELINGS ARE FACTS.**

Whatever you feel is immutable fact to your Unconscious—it is not up for debate. Yet, because most of us have a hard time accepting our feelings, we deny them or tell ourselves they are "wrong." When you say to yourself, "I shouldn't feel that way; that isn't a nice way to feel," or, "I really don't feel attracted to this fabulous man," your Unconscious gets confused. It has a different set of "facts."

In this culture most of us were cut off from our anger. We grew up hearing, "Don't raise your voice to me. Go to your room and don't come out till you can put on a nice face." We have been taught to tell ourselves we do not feel anger, which really means we do not acknowledge or express it.

The result: we store it in our bodies or convert it to depression.

The American Psychiatric Association now asserts that ordinary low-grade depression is no longer a psychiatric disorder because everybody has it. What a comment on our society! It is now normal in America to be depressed. As a culture we have so conspired not to feel, not to express, that all those unacknowledged feelings have turned inward and depressed us.

Anger is the road to your passion. It is your vehicle to be able to take a stand for yourself.

To the extent that you deny anger, you deny life.

Perhaps there were other feelings you were not allowed in your childhood — sadness or fear or hurt. To whatever extent you become able to express them, you will give yourself back the life energy that you have blocked.

**THERE ARE ONLY TWO WAYS FEELINGS CAN GO: IN OR OUT.**

If they are not allowed out, they have to go in. The result can be psychological or stress-related physical symptoms or diseases — headaches, neckaches, backaches, cancer, ulcers, heart problems.

The challenge is to learn effective ways to get your feelings out — not to rail at your boss or your wife, or in any other way hurt yourself, but to find other, neutral ways to get them out and not keep them internalized.

We usually see only two alternatives: to contain our feelings or dump them on someone else. There is a third way. Release them in a controlled way by intentionally crying, yelling, or acting them out.

The key is to express them and not hurt yourself or anyone else in the process.

This is the missing part of our emotional survival training. In self-release the single most important issue is to release, not contain. If you feel hurt, cry. If you feel angry, express it. The challenge is to find a way to express it that doesn't compound your problem.

Later in the chapter I'll be delineating several "Release Valves" to aid in self-expression.

**WHATEVER YOU HAVE NOT BEEN ABLE TO DO IS WHAT YOU MUST LEARN TO DO.**

The challenge is to be authentic with your feelings and not get them crossed. In this culture, boys are taught to deny their pain, so instead of acknowledging hurt, they get mad. Women are taught to deny anger, so instead of getting mad, they get hurt.

A recent study at the University of Michigan revealed that women who express their anger live longer than those who don't. Three times as many women who suppressed their anger died during the course of the study as those who spoke right up. What an incentive to learn to express your true feelings!

To the extent that you are prohibited, you are trapped. To be fully human, you must allow yourself spontaneity across the full spectrum of human-ness.

**GRIEF**

All of us have had losses in our lives, yet we often have not allowed ourselves to fully heal through the grief process. This is true for any loss in your life — love, friends, health, jobs, marriage. Yet, most people do not understand the necessity of moving through the grief process. They block themselves at some point in it by discounting or denying their feelings.

To help you know where you may be unfinished at some stage of a grief in your life, here is the progression which grief takes, explained more fully by Elizabeth Kubler-Ross in her monumental book, "On Death and Dying."

1. **Denial.** "I can't believe this is happening!" My marriage is not failing. My mother is not terminally ill.

2. **Bargaining.** "What can I do so we won't get divorced?" "What do I have to do to keep this job?" "Lord, if you'll just let her live, I'll go to church every Sunday for the rest of my life." Like the magical thinking of childhood, you are in a stage in which you believe that something you DO can change the loss.

3. **Sadness.** You let yourself feel your pain and loss. You let yourself cry. Your heart can

literally ache during this stage. The feeling can come and go. You can be driving down the street feeling OK, and a song comes on the radio and you're destroyed. You can be in a business meeting and hear someone say something that reminds you of a poignant moment, and internally you collapse.

When you are going through these rapid changes you can feel crazy. You aren't crazy. You are just grieving.

4. **Depression.** This is a kind of numbness. You don't care any more. You may sleep a lot, find it hard to get up in the morning, or you may have insomnia. You are not motivated even to see your friends. You lose the luster of life.

5. **Anger.** You get mad about the loss. Perhaps you are angry at the person who died. You have been left, and you did not want the person to leave.

   In marriages that are divorcing this can be a very painful, accusing stage, and can go on for a long time.

6. **Resolution.** The pain has at last been handled. You can talk about it, feel it, without being demolished. This is the all-important stage of forgiveness — forgiveness of self and the

other for all the pain. Then there can be a returning to the belief that no one intended the pain.

Wherever you are stuck in the grieving process, that is the place you must release. If you are still angry at your ex-spouse, then you need to release the anger and forgive. The anger only bonds you two in negative ways.

Everyone in this culture goes through grief, sometimes multiple griefs simultaneously. Obviously, if you have two or three going on at the same time, it is going to further diminish your energy.

If your feelings are not backing up what you want — if you do not have the energy to focus on what you want and deserve — you will not be able to accomplish it.

It has been said by several of my colleagues that all therapy is grief work — grieving for the lost dreams, unanswered hopes, and wounded child feelings in all of us.

**SELF-RELEASE AND SELF-ESTEEM**

The only way to build self-esteem is to have your feelings and your self-worth acknowledged. If that did not happen when you were a child, it needs to happen now.

**Self-release is the hardest issue in Deserve Level.** Positive Self-Talk, learning to say nice things to yourself, is considerably easier. Feelings are much dearer and deeper than thoughts.

You are the person who can make it happen, and you begin by honoring your feelings.

**DIAGNOSTIC EXERCISE:**

Take a moment now to write about your unresolved feelings. State what they are, who is involved in them, and what you tell yourself that keeps you from releasing them.

________________________________________

________________________________________

________________________________________

________________________________________

________________________________________

________________________________________

________________________________________

________________________________________

## RELEASE VALVES: EXERCISES FOR POSITIVE EXPRESSION OF UNRESOLVED FEELINGS

The challenge here is to get out all those feelings that are causing your grief and release the bondage they are keeping you in. If you feel silly or embarrassed as you do them, remind yourself that it's the best way to get rid of the negatives.

### GET OFF MY BACK!

This exercise is done standing up with your knees slightly bent. Your arms are held up and bent at the elbow so your hands are facing each other.

Now, think about the last time someone really made you angry. Think about what they said, focus on your feelings about them and their statements.

Pull back your arms as if you were rowing a boat, and with feeling say, "GET OFF MY BACK!" Keep doing it, at least ten times, until you feel a release from your angry feelings. No wimping out — really try and get them off your back!

## TENNIS RACKET RELEASE

When some people are really angry, they like to hit things. Often what happens is that they contain and contain until they explode and hit whatever is handy. I know a man who lost control in a rage and smashed his fist into a glass coffee table, ending up with 22 stitches in his arm.

That is uncontrolled hitting. The tennis racket release is a wonderful, intentional alternative. All it takes is an old tennis racket and a bed or pile of big pillows.

Mentally place the person you are angry at beside the bed, in a good vantage point to watch you. Now hit the pillows with all your power and tell the person what you are angry about. Keep it simple, one sentence or two at the most. "I'm furious that you left me." "I'm pissed off that you don't want to have sex." Really get into it, say anything you want, and completely release it by whomping the bed with the tennis racket. Find a satisfying rhythm between the words and the racket smacks.

The feeling at the end of this kind of experience is great. Every time I do it I feel emotionally cleansed. And here's the good news: the other guy doesn't even know what I've said. I have released my anger without hurting myself or anyone else, and now I can be rational with the person I'm angry with.

## KILL SOMEONE IN YOUR SHOWER (THE "PSYCHO" RELEASE

This release is performed in the comfort of your own shower. Turn on the water and get your wash cloth and soap. Now, think of all the negative things you want to say to the person you're angry with. Picture them there and say anything you want. Throw the wash cloth, yell, cuss, toss the soap at them. Then wash off the rest of your anger and step out physically and emotionally clean.

## CLOWN YOUR WAY THROUGH

Many people find a good release in laughing away their tensions. If that appeals to you, another technique when you're feeling sad or angry is to laugh it away. One helpful way is with the clown technique.

If you've had a bad day and are frustrated and upset, get in your car and pull out your "clown nose." Put in on and casually drive home waving at people as you pass them. You can't stay in a funk for very long with a clown nose on your face.

## TEA AND SYMPATHY
## or
## WINE AND BITCHING

If you're feeling depressed or low, one of the best strategies is real contact with people you love. Your best friend, a close work associate, a family member — someone you can predict will be kind and care about your pain.

Share with your friend as deeply as you can what you are really feeling and let them give back their love and concern. If they shift into advice, remind them that what you want is a caring, listening ear — sympathy and support.

## COMMUNICATION WITH OTHERS

An important issue in Self-Release is our relationships. All of us are here because other people have loved us, and none of us is going anywhere without other people loving and believing in us.

We have relationships everywhere — in work, in friendship, at home — and when things are not working in some of your relationships, communication is often a major factor. How does communication in relationships get bogged down?

The single most destructive interaction in human relations is what has been called the RESCUE TRIANGLE. It occurs in intimate relationships, in the workplace, in management. It is a particular form of negative communication patterns and role assumptions, based on unhealthy dependency, which keeps all its players frustrated and resentful.

Here is how the triangle looks:

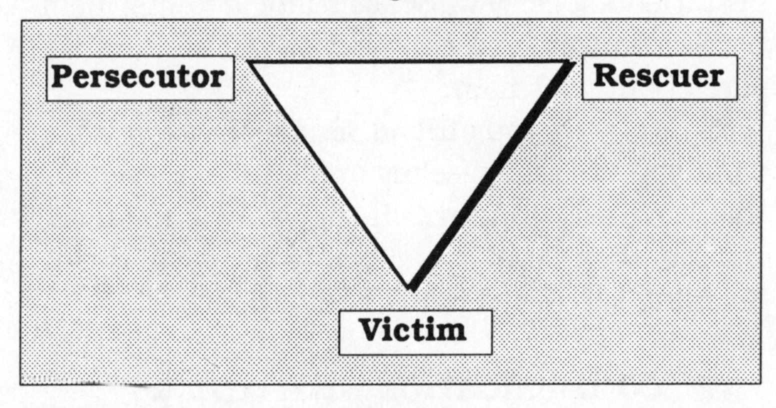


1) **Rescuers** are people who are over-responsible. They give 90% and get back 10%. They do not say NO when they don't want to do things, because they are afraid of appearing selfish. Their NEED is to give and nurture and take care of other people. They do not ask for what they want, because they see as their JOB to be there for others, ever ready and ever responsive. They do not set firm boundaries for the same reasons.

Most of us have been trained that it is more blessed to give than to receive. The problem wth being in a determined Rescuer position is that it is obligatory. Rescuers do not see an acceptable alternative. Often they are not giving because they want to, but because they think they SHOULD.

Rescuers tell themselves, "No matter what I feel, what I want or need, what is going on with me, I have no right to myself. I am here to cater to and give to you." "You" is virtually everyone: husband, wife, corporation, children, parents, friends.

2) **Victims** are people who are under-responsible. They invite and need Rescuers to tell them what to do and rescue them. They tend to be passive and don't know what they want. They tend not to take responsibility for themselves, nor indeed for what they create in their world. They look to other people to make things right for them. They have a sense of being powerless, unable to do things or create positive outcomes in their lives. They believe life has victimized them. They feel helpless and hopeless and look to assign blame for their feelings on someone else. "They made me ..." is their emotional litany.

Each of us is sometimes a true victim — that is, caught in a situational bind not of our own making. A friend really can find that his battery has died overnight, and will call and ask you for a ride. If, however, he has a different broken-car reason to call you every day, he is playing in the Rescue Triangle. He is not taking responsibility for getting his own car in order — or his life, or his financial condition, or whatever "emergency" he creates to "need" you to rescue him.

Let's observe a Rescue Triangle in action at a family dinner table (which is often where it originates). This scenario happened every night in my family around the important issue of iced tea.

I put sugar in my iced tea. Dad, coming from Persecutor position, glowers and says, putting me in the Victim role, "You are going to die of diabetes. There is diabetes in this family, and you are going to die of it."

Because this happens every night, I open my science book and say "But we're studying about diabetes in school, Dad. It says here that it takes a lot more than just sugar to cause diabetes."

Dad totally discounts my source and continues to rant at me about the sugar in my tea. He also tells me not to get smart with him.

And who comes in at this point? Mom, in the Rescuer Position. "There, there, honey, it's

OK, your Dad doesn't mean to be angry." Dad turns on her and says, "That's the trouble with this family, there is NO DISCIPLINE, and it's YOUR FAULT!" Mom can now play Victim.

I come back in and say to Mom, "Come on, Mom, let's go play Scrabble together." I rescue her and we leave.

Who won? Nobody! We bought a ticket and took the ride around the entire Rescue Triangle, and everybody was left with bad feelings.

The irony of the Rescue Triangle is that all people can, at some time or another, play every position. If you rescue long enough, you become a victim. You also can move into the role of Persecutor.

That bears repeating. **Once you buy a ticket to play Rescue, you eventually go around the whole cycle.**

This is a relationship based on need. Victims need Rescuers (and vice versa). So, what happens when Victims start feeling better about themselves? One of two things. Maybe they say to the Rescuer, "Thanks so much, but I don't need you any more. I will always remember how you were there for me during and after my divorce, but I am going off now to marry Harry/Sally." Or else they might get angry and say, "I never needed you in the first place. You're driving me crazy. Bug off!" In other words, they can get angry, which enables them to play Persecutor.

3) **Persecutors** are people who are angry, frustrated, fed up. They are frequently Rescuers who have had it and flipped into the Persecutor position. When a Rescuer moves into Persecutor s/he might say, "I'm mad at you, I've had it with you. After all I've done for you, how can you treat me like this?" They are often quite justified in their anger, because they have over-given and over-done. Now, ask yourself: What happens inside nice people after they persecute? Exactly: They feel guilty! Guilt then builds a bridge from Persecutor back to Rescuer, and they get to go on another ride. "I was so awful, why did I act like that. This time I am going to be really nice. I'll give even more, delay my own gratification and take care of that other person."

Rescue is the most predominate game of negative communication played in this culture. It is rampant, not only with couples and families, but in the marketplace. Think of how a lot of corporations are run — to say nothing of small-shop entrepeunerships —

and you will be able to write your own scenarios to illustrate the Rescue game.

That is not to say that all giving is a game of Rescue. When you want to give to somebody, as long as you take responsibility for the giving and take care of yourself in the process, you are all right. Even then, however, notice if you are the giver a disproportionate amount of the time.

Rescuers are doing it out of a sense of obligation, because they think they have to, as if it were their consecretated life work.

Ironically, it is the person you give too much to who ends up leaving you for someone else (in business or romance), or at the very least exploiting you. If a real estate agent gives 150% to a prospective buyer, he is exactly the one who will end up buying through another agent. It is the long-suffering supergivers who often get left in mid-life for another woman/man. If you play rescuer, you will end up as victim.

How do you avoid taking the ride?

1) Know what you want and how to ask for it.

2) Do not give more than your fair share. Sometimes 60/40, but NOT 90/10.

3) Ask for people to give back. This is true in any relationship, personal or business. If they don't they are not invested in the relationship, and you need to know that. In sales, there are customers none of us can afford to have. They are the ones that sap your time and energy and never give back by buying. Or if they do buy they are endlessly demanding.

4) Remember that good relationships are a dance for two. If you are taking all the steps, the other person cannot dance with you. Take a step, and then wait and let your partner take a step. Give her or him a chance — don't preempt his move with your impatience or your impulse to over-give.

5) In personal relationships, do not allow yourself to fall in love with someone's potential. Rocks have potential! If you do, chances are you have found an under-responsible Victim for you to Rescue ("surely the love of a good woman will turn him around / open him up to intimacy / show him how good life can be"). Fall in love with reality.

6) If you find yourself really indignant or resentful (at a lover, friend, boss), notice that

the same principles apply. You have probably been setting yourself up to play the role of Rescuer/Martyr. A clue is your response to a phone message from them. If you hear it and go, "Oh no, not him!" — BINGO! you are in the Rescue Triangle.

7. Say NO to what you really do not want to do. It will not turn out well if you say Yes when you mean No.

## JUST SAY NO

Ann tells a story that rings familiar bells with many of us. She returned home from a week-long business trip, worn out, and was talking with her husband about plans for the evening. She said, "I'm exhausted. All I want to do is be entertained. Let's go to a movie."

He said, "OK." She went on to suggest a funny movie she had read about and once again he said, "OK."

Sitting in the movie, Ann was happy as a lark with her popcorn in one hand, a Diet Coke in the other, just enjoying the experience. Then she began to pick up negative vibes from her husband. She ignored them, hoping they would go away.

After the movie they went out to eat. All through dinner he was very quiet. Finally she said, "What's wrong?" and he responded, "Nothing." Finally she said, "What is the problem, what have I done that is irritating you?"

He said, "I didn't want to go to the movies, and I really didn't want to go to that movie!"

"Why did you?"

"I wanted to make sure you had a good evening!"

How many of us have tried to make sure someone else is happy and done something we didn't want to do? And in the process, made everyone miserable.

The Rescue Ride starts out with the best of intentions and blows up in our faces.

**BOUNDARIES**

Boundaries are the limits to which you are willing to go. We show healthy boundaries to others when we decline to be exploited.

Set your boundaries and stick with them. That means setting boundaries within yourself, because these old behavior patterns can be addictive.

Communication is not just inter-personal (you with others), it is also intra-personal (you with yourself). You can be kind but firm with yourself about not allowing your old patterns to keep running you, particularly if they keep hurting you.

I've had this experience in my personal relationships. I have a tendency, as do many women, to want to accommodate to men. If a man I'm relating to is unhappy with me, I feel very uncomfortable. I start feeling that I'm bad or wrong because of my point of view or behavior. I begin to give myself away to appease the man, do what he wants, and ignore my own needs.

Breaking my boundaries because of someone else's displeasure is ultimately self-defeating. I end up resenting him and myself. Nobody wins.

**DIAGNOSTIC EXERCISE:**

Write down ways you have allowed yourself to buy a ticket onto the Rescue Ride. Note what roles you have played in certain relationships, how your selection process ignored warning signals, and what you would do differently today if you could do it over.

______________________________________________

______________________________________________

______________________________________________

______________________________________________

______________________________________________

______________________________________________

Now that you have told yourself the truth about your feelings, you can learn how to defeat that nemesis of high achievers: perfectionism. You may think it has helped you get where you are today. Actually, it has limited you more than it has aided you. The next chapter explains this paradox more fully.

# •10•

# Self-Nurturing

*"People create the reality they need in order to discover themselves."*

— *Ernest Becker*

As I've gone around the country teaching seminars on Deserve Level psychology, I have noticed that it's very easy for most of us to point a finger at ourselves or others and say, "That's how you messed up. No wonder your life isn't working."

The critical and negative voice sings so readily in our heads.

However you have been sabotaging yourself, it's what you needed to do to grow and learn. You didn't do it consciously to hurt yourself. It becomes the standard bearer to your new sense of self. It is the light that signals an end to the darkness, if you pay attention.

Sabotages are your unconscious mind telling you, "I'm not ready. I need more time, support, or permission to achieve that goal I so desire."

Knowing that, it's important to embrace rather than abuse that from your inner self. But how?

One of our hardest challenges to self-growth is learning to nurture and love ourselves. Most of us grew up putting ourselves down for every mistake and minor error. We learned it at home. Father may have criticized us because we did not clean up the kitchen or do that homework. Teachers, friends, and siblings all had their part in pointing out our limitations. Now, as adults, we don't need them any more. We have learned our lessons well. We are our own best self-critics.

The development of a self-critical attitude is learned very early.

Four-year-old Johnny is outside playing with his puppy. It is a lovely spring morning and they are having a fine time, jumping and chasing each other. Like most children, Johnny isn't very attentive to details. He leaves the gate open and the puppy runs out.

Crying, he goes to his mother. "My puppy dog ran away!" His mother has had a horrible day with problem after problem. This presents one more frustration than she can handle. She says angrily,

"You bad boy! How many times have I told you to shut that gate?"

Now take the same situation with different characters. Four-year-old Steve comes running, crying, to tell his mother the puppy has run away. This mother says, "Oh, honey, you must feel awful to lose your puppy dog. Let's go see if we can't find him."

Johnny's mother criticized and added guilt to his pain. For him it was a lesson self-rejection.

Steve, who was nurtured in his sadness and then helped to fix the problem, learned a positive alternative.

Both children feel sad at the loss of the puppy, but Johnny gets sadness plus guilt, which equals depression. Depression is not naturally healing. If Johnny learns to put himself down for every error, he can stay depressed and critical of himself all his life.

Steve also feels sad, but he has the support of his mother. Sadness plus nurturing equals grief, which <u>is</u> naturally healing. After a period of grieving, he will return to normal, his Deserve Level intact, and he will not be stamped with blame.

One incident won't make you feel self-critical, but hundreds of incidents do create deep personal doubts and low Deserve Level.

The emotional equation looks like this:

| Feels | Receives | Emotional Response |
| --- | --- | --- |
| Sad | Criticism and blame | Low Deserve Level and Depression |
| Sad | Nurturing | OK Deserve Level and Grief |

Most of us have been raised on a steady diet of self-criticism rather than nurturing. We continue this tradition and treat the four-year-old in us in very critical ways.

## CHANGING SELF-CRITICISM TO SELF-NURTURING

Dr. Eric Berne developed a model of human interaction known as Transactional Analysis (TA) to simplify psychoanalysis for public understanding. Berne taught that a person is made up of three ego states — Parent, Adult, and Child. No matter what the age or life experience, each of us has a Parent, Adult, and Child ego state.

The "Shoulds" and "Oughts" reside in the Parent ego state. "You should brush your teeth." "You ought to exercise." The Parent delivers all the instructions and "how-to's," along with judgments and opinions. The Parent has two different aspects, the Nurturing Parent and the Critical Parent.

The Adult ego state deals basically with facts. Not much emotion, just plain facts. "How old are you?" "What time is it?"

The Child ego state harbors our feelings. When we feel sadness, anger, joy, or hurt, we are in our Child ego state.

Self-criticism occurs when there is an event, feeling, or thought the Parent deems inappropriate and the Critical Parent comes on strong with negative messages: "You're so stupid, how many times do I have to tell you not to do that!" "You're selfish for wanting that. Stop it!" We all have our favorite negative fiction that we hear when we are self-critical. The Child in us feels shamed and blamed. The outcome blocks us in our movements, humiliates us for wanting something, or embarrasses us for our feelings. We shut down emotionally and are at war inside ourselves. Usually the Child in us feels hurt, angry, and sad.

One of the most frequent parent criticisms is that we are selfish or want too much. Who has not been told, "Your eyes are bigger than your stomach! You can't eat all that food!"

Some parents call their children selfish for their every want or desire. This criticism surfaces for big or little wants, from something as small as a dime-store toy to a car. The term selfish is used as a club to humiliate or evoke guilt. Alexander Lowen says in Bioenergetics, "When children are told that they are asking for too much, the parents are putting them down. A child never asks for too much, it asks for what it wants. 'Too much' is an adult evaluation that serves to make the child feel guilty for wanting."

This child grows up. This child is you or me — and when we want something, we immediately begin to feel guilty, selfish, and undeserving. We curb our simplest wants out of fear of disapproval, our own or someone else's. We limit our Deserve Level.

Self-nurturing offers the alternative to chronic self-criticism. To get a feel for your own ability to criticize or nurture yourself, close your eyes and fantasize for a minute after you read these instructions. See the last incident of something you did that you didn't like. For example, you locked yourself out of the house, forgot to enter a check, lost something of value. Now listen to what you said to yourself. Have a dialogue between the Critical Parent part of yourself and the Child part.

Do you call yourself names, berate yourself, put yourself down? How is the four-year-old self feeling? Somewhat angry and depressed? Ashamed or hopeless? This is the dialogue that happens when you haven't lived up to your own expectations. You haven't been perfect.

Now try a different approach. Think of the same incident and see yourself as a four-year-old. Pretty cute kid, huh? This little person didn't mean to mess up. He/she is just learning or a little careless. Certainly excusable behavior. Be the child and share your feelings with the Nurturing Parent. "I feel stupid (sad, hurt, angry) that I __________." Elaborate on how you feel about the situation. Then let your Nurturing Parent come in and say, "I hear you. I understand that you feel __________. I'm with you and I'll support you. I love you." Continue this conversation for as long as possible. Nurturing means unconditional support for your being and your personhood. Because it affirms that you are lovable, it raises your self-esteem.

After you have finished this exercise, compare your bodily feelings betwen self-criticism and self-nurturing. There should be a great difference in your feelings of stress and tension between the two dialogues.

Let me give you a step-by-step account of learning self-nurturing. This dialogue came from a session with Barbara, a very successful therapist who has helped thousands of people overcome their emotional problems. In her own life she struggles with a phobia about making speeches. This is a dialogue she had between her Critical Parent, Inner Child, and Nurturing Parent. See if it sounds familiar.

**Critical Parent:** "You can't do any speeches. You don't know anything. They will all laugh at you. Who do you think you are?"

**Child (crying):** "I know you're right. I can't do it. I don't have anything to say. I'm scared I'll mess it up."
(Makes an intentional switch to the Nurturing Parent.)

**Nurturing Parent** (soothingly): "I hear you. I understand you're scared. I believe in you. I'll help you through this."

**Child (angrily):** "I don't believe you. You've never helped me before. Why should you be there now?"

**Nurturing Parent:** "I understand that you're angry, and you have a right to be. You're right. I haven't been very supportive. I intend to change and stop criticizing you and start supporting you."

**Child:** "I don't know — you sound good, but can I trust you?

**Nurturing Parent:** "Just watch my behavior and give me a chance. I believe you can give speeches. You're bright and have lots of good information for people."

**Child:** "I feel better. I sure like it when you don't verbally beat me up."

**Nurturing Parent:** "I don't want to any longer. I love you and want the best for you."

**Child (heavy sigh):** "Thanks."

Faries McDaniel, M.S.S.W., developed this model for Interpsychic Nurturing. It applies to self-nurturing and nurturing of others, and can be used at any time.

**THE SELF-NURTURING PROCESS**

1) To begin, state in the first person how you are feeling, from the Child ego state: "I'm hurting." "I'm worthless." "I'm stupid." Explore and encourage verbal owning of feelings.

2) After this has gone on for a while, ask yourself what the Nurturing Parent in you would like to say to the Hurt Child. It might be something like, "I like you just the way you are." "You're okay." "I'm here for you, I'll

take care of you." "I understand how you feel, and we're going to make it through."

3) Continue a dialogue between the Hurt Child and the Nurturing Parent. When you can feel (or hear, or see in changed body position) that the Child is feeling better, then to to the Adult ego state.

4) With the Child feelings soothed, the Adult assesses the situation, looks at the facts, considers alternatives, and makes a decision.

5) The Adult says in the first person, "I will do ..." "I have decided to ..." Now check out how you feel. You should be more relaxed and ready to make a good decision.

This self-nurturing exercise offers an excellent way to practice building up your self-esteem. Every night before you go to sleep, grab a pillow and hold it close to you. Pretend this is you as a four-year-old child. Let yourself tell you the feelings you are having: I'm scared or anxious, or whatever. Then see and feel your own Nurturing Parent come in and love that Inner Child. This exercise has soothed many a painful night for me.

Nurturing is a learned art. Most of us grew up feeling heavily criticized by well-intentioned grown-ups, and we became extremely self- and other-critical. To turn these negative patterns around takes tenacity and a devotion to the practice of not beating ourselves up!

Believing that I'm not such a bad person has helped me to keep myself committed to my own self-nurturing. I would never find the level of imperfections in others as awful as I do my own. Finally I decided to give myself a break and nurture my mess-ups and mistakes rather than be self-abusive. Guess what? I feel so much better about myself, and consequently don't create as many problems as I used to.

Right before completing my master's thesis I had an occasion to use my newly-developed self-nurturing skills. As I started to go in to give my oral presentation, panic hit me. What if I couldn't remember anything? What if I failed? Two years of hard work gone down the drain! I was working up a good anxiety attack when I remembered the nurturing techniques. I went into the bathroom, sat on the toilet, and talked softly to that scared little kid in my stomach. "I love you, it's okay. You'll make it through. They won't kill you." Strange as it may sound, it really helped. I walked out relieved — and then saw my major professor standing at the sink. She smiled and said to me, "You're right, we won't kill you." Amazingly, I passed anyway.

This story of my master's thesis anxiety points out a significant fact:

**The curse of high achievers is perfectionism. The curse of perfectionism is ignoring the 95% that is right and focusing on the 5% that is not.**

We have a tendency to see the flaws, what's not done or finished in our business or personal life.

**If you pay attention to the kinds of messages even the most well-intentioned families send, it becomes clear where we learned to accentuate the negative.**

When the ratio is more like 20/80 — when everything seems to be going wrong — it is even harder for us to show compassion and friendship to ourselves.

The blunt truth is this: if we treated others the way we often treat ourselves, we wouldn't have any friends.

Fortunately for our friends, we usually know how to be supportive to them. The challenge is learning to do the same for ourselves.

It is easy to cheer for ourselves when things are going well. The challenge of self-nurturing is to learn to be loving to ourselves when things are <u>not</u> going well, when we are not perfect.

One of the best rules for managing salespeople is paradoxical:

Love them when they're down and goose them to greatness when they're up.

This is the opposite of what we usually do to ourselves. When our success is down and things are not going well, the temptation is to beat yourself up, tell yourself you are not any good.

That approach is not only unkind, it does not work. It simply drives the cycle down further.

When the going gets tough is when it is most important to nurture yourself.

Nurturing is not about making excuses, rationalizing, blaming others. It is about comforting and respecting yourself.

If you can be loving, appreciative, and concerned about yourself and others, you can lift your energy. When you are doing well is when you can challenge yourself to do even better. That is when you have the energy to keep creating. When you are down, you don't.

Remember that we are not talking about accepting an unwanted situation. Self-nurturing does not mean accepting a 40% drop in sales with equanimity — it means accepting yourself even when those sales are down.

If you keep telling yourself, "I've got to be better, I'm not doing it right, I'm not making things happen," you predict and project from negative energy.

Self-acceptance means acknowledging your own efforts and energy, what you have done to try to make the desired outcome happen.

The difference is in our own self-dialogue. The difference is between a nurturing or a critical comment, a loving or an abusive action.

One of my most instructive lessons in self-nurturing came when I made an error. I was asked to appear on a local TV show to discuss a seminar I was conducting. It was 1979, and the other guest on the program was Barbara Bush. She was beginning the tour around the country promoting George for his 1989 presidential bid. I dimly knew who George Bush was but was confused about her relationship to him.

She and I chatted for a minute or two, and then I said, "It's so nice of you to go around the country promoting your son for the presidency."

There was a heavy silence, and then she replied, "I'm his wife, not his mother." I gasped at what I'd said, hastily made an excuse that I had to go to the bathroom. I sat down in one of those small meditation booths and tried to put my life back together, because I knew I'd just made the dumbest remark of my life. So I nurtured myself and reminded myself that my intent had been positive. My information was wrong, but my heart had been in the right place.

**EXPERIENTIAL EXERCISE**

You can experience the difference between nurturance and criticalness with an exercise in imagination.

Close your eyes and pretend that your mind is a radio, and you can choose your station. Actually visualize a radio on the table in front of you.

Turn the dial to the station you usually listen to. Maybe it is full of self-criticism, or the kind of pseudo-acceptance that sounds supportive but really has a zinger in it. "Not bad, but you ought to be doing a whole lot better." Listen carefully to that same old static that is so familiar.

Now reach out and turn the dial to a new, positive station. Literally see your hand on the dial, feel it turn, until you tune in a new station. This one has only positive, nurturing things to say about you — not about the situation, but about you. "I'm with you. I believe in you. You are a good person. You can get through this." Listen for a while to these nurturing, positive statements.

Now turn the dial back to the old critical station, and feel in your body how you feel when you hear it again.

Once again, turn back to the positive station. Breathe deeply. Feel how you feel as you listen to that.

That experience happens in your own unconscious all the time, particularly when you are going into situations that require change, that require you to do something different — like grow and develop.

We all resist and have trouble with change. We may want it, but we have trouble with it. One of the important issues as you set about increasing your Deserve Level is to notice that resistance, that fear. When you start to move toward getting more of what you want, be self-nurturing instead of self-critical. Nobody ascends like a rocket — we all take a couple of steps forward, then a step back. To keep your energy going in a positive direction, you have to develop the ability to be self-nurturing.

This is not an easy process to master, when you have been trained to believe that you achieve by harassing and criticizing yourself.

Another way you can keep yourself stuck in negatives is by not forgiving yourself or others. Forgiving yourself means releasing the blame and regret over your actions or feelings.

Feeling guilty or angry about someone or some experience bonds you to them in a negative cohesion. It's time to let go of these unresolved feelings.

## FORGIVENESS EXERCISE

Sit quietly with your eyes closed. Breathe very deeply. Now see yourself going down a flight of stairs. There are 30 steps. Slowly count them down, one at a time, until you reach the bottom.

At the bottom you enter a lovely room that is filled with a wonderful white light. Take a seat and see yourself talking with the person that you haven't let go of. Say everything you want to say about your hurt, frustration, or rejected feelings.

After you've said all you need to say, tell the person, "I forgive and release you. I forgive and release myself." See the two of you enveloped in the white light, and leave in peace.

Creating a nurturing environment within yourself can be greatly enhanced by having a support system that reinforces your needs. The next chapter tells you how to implement that experience in your life.

# •11•

# Self-Support
# Weaving your Sustaining Network

"I want to love you without judging, join you without invading, invite you without demanding, leave you without guilt, criticize you without blaming, and help you without insulting. If I can have the same from you then we can truly meet and enrich each other."

*- Virginia Satir*

"What is real?" asked the Rabbit.

"Real isn't how you are made," said the Skin Horse. "It's a thing that happens to you. When a child loves you for a long, long time, not just to play with, but really loves you, then you become Real."

"Does it hurt?" asked the Rabbit.

"Sometimes," said the skin horse, for he was always truthful. "When you are Real you don't mind being hurt."

"Does it happen all at once, like being wound up," he asked, "or bit by bit?"

"It doesn't happen all at once," said the Skin Horse. "You become. It takes a long time. That's why it doesn't often happen to people who break easily, or have sharp edges, or who have to be carefully kept. Generally by the time you are Real, most of your hair has been loved off, and your eyes drop out and you get loose in the joints and very shabby. But these things don't matter at all, because once you are Real you can't be ugly, except to those people who don't understand."

This lovely quote from The Velveteen Rabbit sums up our need for love and support. To "up" our Deserve Level and get what we want in life, we need the love and support of other people. Too often we don't allow this need for support to be expressed.

We live in a world where the pioneer mentality reigns. We are trained to be rugged individuals who take care of ourselves, are self-reliant and completely self-sustaining. Many times I've had people in therapy who have said, "I really don't want to be here. I thought I could handle this myself." These folks believe that seeking help, support, or education is admitting weakness and failure. Their belief system contains the thought that they ought to be able to handle everything without assistance.

The reality of the world we live in is very different. We have moved to greater and greater diversification in all areas of life. That means the era of total self-sufficiency is over (if it ever existed), and we need each other to create an integrated life. This mutual interdependence is the basis for our technology, culture, and psychology. We need support from each other for our very existence.

What do I mean when I say support?

You are here because someone has loved you. As children we ran to our parents when we needed psychological support. Our mothers primarily were the grounding forces when we felt emotionally overwhelmed. When hurt, angry, sad, we ran to them for support and reassurance.

If we were lucky enough to have "good enough" nurturing, we felt loved and lovable. We had an emotional foundation under us that we could depend on. If this support was consistent, we learned to rely on this source of nurturance, to count on its being there.

That let us be free to go out on our own, knowing there would be a safe harbor to return to if we should need it.

The challenge is to create support systems for yourself, to draw from your friends and mentors, to have others besides your spouse or sweetheart. Being another person's sole emotional support is too big a burden to put on a relationship.

"To give is to receive. That's the law of Love. Under this law, when we give our love away to others we gain, and what we give we simultaneously receive. This law is based on abundance."

This quotation from Gerald Jampolsky's best seller, Love Is Letting Go of Fear, expresses the wonderful duality of suport and personal giving. If we give support or love, we then receive it back. Jampolsky says,

"The law of the world is based on a belief in scarcity. That means that whenever we give something to someone we lose it. We must then constantly be on the lookout to get our needs met. We must search and search to fill our empty well. We live in a belief of emptiness and constant need. We try to fill those needs through getting other people to love us or give to us.

When we expect others to satisfy our desires we are constantly disappointed. They never do it right!

When we are feeling depressed and finding someone to give us love is not really the solution, what is necessary is to give love to someone else. That love is then simultaneously given to ourselves. The other person doesn't have to change or give us anything.

The world's distorted concept is that you have to get other people's love before you can feel love within. The las of love is different fro the world's law. The law of love is that you are love, and that as you give love to others you teach yourself what you are.

It's not charity on my part to offer forgiveness and love to others. Rather it's the only way I can accept love for myself."

Every one of us will hit nights of black despair. There will be dark times in our lives. It's then that you need your friends.

It isn't easy to feel vulnerable. When you feel vulnerable you may do a great deal of scurrying around to cover the feelings. That is when you need a friend you can call who believes in you.

Far from being a sign of weakness, the truth is that asking and receiving support from others is part of being a strong and self-sufficient person. Really strong people value themselves and don't like feeling hurt or depressed. They take care of their human needs. They ask for support and aren't critical of themselves when they need it.

As you are building your support system, it is important to have friends who are living in the ways that you want to live. The friends we associate with invite us to their level of experiencing life. If your friends are all fast-track professionals who are proving themselves in their corporate worlds — and you want to get off that train, have a baby, and enjoy life's softer side — they will subtly or even directly tell you to live by their rules. You may find yourself "out of sync" with them and feeling lonely.

That is a clue that you need the addition of others who share your current life view. It is difficult for all of us to be empathetic or supportive of someone whose lifestyle is radically different from ours. That's why we need affiliations with friends in our particular life phase. Such friends can affirm what we're doing and what we believe in, and can encourage us to become what we want to be.

We must all be prodded to greatness. None of us will go there without resistance. That's what a good support system does for you. It believes in you so completely that you are moved to action.

One of our struggles can be in assessing who in our system is helping us move forward and who is holding us back. Old friends from college can go in different directions, develop different values as the years go by. They may still care, but your life paths are different now, have simply grown apart. No one is wrong, you are just no longer right for each other.

The same experience can happen in marriages and families. If your support system has become critical or negative about what you want in your life, ask them to be more respectful and supportive. If you allow the people closest to you to undermine your values, you will get depressed, frustrated, defeated. Ultimately, we educate other people about how we expect to be treated.

Doesn't it make sense to gravitate toward people with whom you have mutual respect, who are doing what you want to be doing, people you admire and believe in? They will make it easier for you. That is the whole premise of mentoring or networking — to have people help you along the path.

When I was a beginning speaker I went to the National Speakers Association meeting, where I met a famous speaker, Joe Charbonneau. He was giving a presentation that captivated the audience with his humor, wisdom, and his own personal power. I sat there and thought, "Gee, I wish I could be as good as he is." After the presentation I gathered my courage and approached him. I said, "I'm just beginning my career and would appreciate any help. Would you listen to this demonstration tape of one of my seminars and give me some feedback?"

He smiled and said, "I'd be glad to." He opened his briefcase and put in the tape, and I saw that he had about a hundred others in there as well. I thought, "Well, that's that. He'll never have time to listen to my tape."

Five days later he called me from Cleveland, Ohio, and said, "Sit down, I have five pages of notes on how you can become a great speaker!"

I felt like crying. I didn't expect such a supportive, helpful response.

Joe taught me something very important that day. I had debated whether to ask for his help and expertise. I didn't want to bother him or intrude. All those reasons for sabotaging my needs went through my mind, when the truth was, if he didn't want to help me he wouldn't have done anything. By asking I was giving him a gift to enjoy himself through being supportive.

As he said, "One of the best aspects of being a speaker is to watch and encourage new talent. I remember when I was just starting, and I want to pass on all the encouragement I received."

A motivational speaker tells the story about being on his return flight from giving a speech. The man sitting next to him, when learning what he did for a living, said, "Aaah, that motivational stuff doesn't last. You get yourself all pumped up for a while and then it wears off."

A passing flight attendant overheard him and said, "Well, a bath doesn't last either, but it's still a good idea."

If you think about it, food doesn't last either. Exercise doesn't last. Everything in life needs to be renewed and nurtured. We feel hungry, we eat, we feel full, and in due time we get hungry again. Life is pulsation.

The same thing is true about motivation. It is important that we keep motivating ourselves and others, because we all run out of it.

**Motivation is the dynamic tension between the push of discomfort and the pull of hope.** You have to have some discomfort to be motivated. You have to want something, to yearn for some desired goal. There has to be some discomfort about where you are before you are motivated to change your life. You have to want to lose ten pounds, make more money, or live more serenely.

At the same time you have to have some hope. You have to believe it is possible to change, that what you want is attainable. You have to know it's possible by experience. You know someone who has lost ten pounds or made more money or become serene.

You need to have discomfort and hope in balance, with approximately equal amounts of each, to be motivated.

We aren't always feeling balanced or motivated. Sometimes we have too much discomfort and too little hope. What happens when the scales tip in that direction? We're grumpy, unhappy with how our life is going. This becomes the usual gripe session. "Nothing's right, the economy stinks, my love life is a mess."

What we need at that time is hope. We need to be loved through our despair and discomfort. If we go to a friend and explain our problems he says, "Yeah, the world's a mess, no one can do well in this economy, just forget women, it never works out anyway," he has given us more discomfort and pushed us farther into the motivational slump.

We can get out of balance on the other side as well. We can have <u>too much hope and too little discomfort.</u> I know this sounds like "Margaritas on the beach," but it doesn't work out that way. Too much hope looks more like inertia, being in a rut, not feeling challenged about your career or love life. It's all very predictable and routine. You'll hear it when someone is talking about himself and making statements like, "I've been in insurance sales for twenty years. I now what to do. I'm doing okay, it's steady income."

What's missing is the excitement, the juice, the passion. It's all gotten routine and deadly dull. So, what's needed? Some discomfort to realign the motivational balance.

None of us get out of our ruts gracefuly or easily. We need to be challenged to do something to bring back our feelings of life and passion.

Mid-life crisis is just such a shaking up. Whatever you're doing in mid-life, you want to do the opposite. If you're married, you want to be single; if you're single, you want to be married. If you have kids, you want to be rid of them; if you don't, you want them. It's a great time for reflection and reassessment of what is really important to you.

The formula is very simple. Whatever side you have the most of, you need more of the other side in order to get remotivated. Too much discomfort: get hope. Too much hope: get discomfort.

As a friend or manager, understanding this motivational equation can give you the answer of what to do when someone comes to you in a crisis.

Marilyn Schwartz, a columnist for the Dallas Morning News, wrote an article that illustrates the curative effect of support and encouragement when you're in high discomfort.

"Debra Fowler's parents took her to dinner last month for her 28th birthday. At the end of the meal she received what was heralded as a 'very special fortune cookie.'

"'The waiter told me that on a birthday,' she says, 'the fortune inside the cookie comes twice over. Then he handed me a cookie.

"'I opened it and had to laugh. It read, "Bad luck will go away, god luck will enter your life." That was at least appropriate. If anybody ever needed good luck, I did.'

"Debra explains that in the past three years she has lost a job, gotten a divorce, and survived a serious illness.

"'I've been pretty down,' she says. 'I got so negative that I just didn't believe anything was ever going to go right for me again. I knew my parents were worried about me because they made a big fuss over the fortune. They said I should take it as a sign.'

"Debra says she laughed and told them is was just a piece of paper.

"But the very next day, Debra began to change her mind. She got a call from a man who said she had just won a new TV set in a grocery store giveaway.

"'I told him I was sure I had never even signed up. But later, my mother told me she'd written in my name when she signed up. The TV was delivered the next day.'

"A day later, Debra received a bouquet of flowers. The card was signed, 'An admirer.'

"That same week, her apartment manager told her that for being such a trustworthy tenant, she was going to get special mail service for one day.

"Within the next week, her best friend from Houston flew in to surprise her. She went out on two very pleasant blind dates. And, while having her hair cut, she was told she would get a free facial as part of a salon promotion.

"'Every time I told my mother what was happening,' Debra says, 'she'd just say, "I told you the fortune would come true."'

"Debra says that, by this time, she was sure her good luck was being 'helped along.'

"'No one is that lucky,' she says.

"Boxes of candy were left at her doorstep, She went to dinner with friends and a bottle of champagne was brought to her table with another note that read, 'An admirer.'

"'Everyone I knew seemed to be in on this month of surprises,' Debra says. 'I kept saying, "This is silly. Enough is enough. I'm getting embarrassed."' But the surprises kept coming. I complained, but I really couldn't wait to see what would come next.'

"One night during happy hour Debra ordered a margarita, and the drink arrived with a gift-wrapped package.

"'Inside were instructions to finish my drink and then to proceed to a certain Mexican restaurant,' Debra says.

"When she walked into the restaurant, she was ushered to a party in a private room.

"There were all her friends, her parents, her brother and sister — all the people, it turned out, who had helped bring about the 'good luck.'

"Debra explains that just one year ago, she was in the hospital and no one knew whether she would recover.

"'I got better, but I just couldn't seem to get back my good spirits. I felt so bleak. I realized my friends and my family found a way to reach me. I can't tell you how much good this did for me.

"'It wasn't just the gifts that got to me. It was all the time and effort they spent to make me feel special again.'

"Debra's mother, Jenny Kirkpatrick, who lives in Irving, stood up at the party and made a speech. 'I told Debra,' she says, 'that this was to be a lesson to her. Sometimes you can't wait for good luck to find you. Sometimes you have to make it yourself.'

"Then she proposed a toast and added one more piece of motherly advice.

"'I hope you learned the lesson well, Debra,' she said. 'Because from now on, when you open a fortune cookie — you're on your own.'"

**THE STROKE ECONOMY**

Another important component of our support needs is a positive stroke system. The expression "strokes" comes from Transactional Analysis. By definition, strokes are any form of positive or negative attention, given as a form of acknowledgement.

To the extent that we get positive strokes in our lives, we feel energized. To the extent that we get negative strokes, we feel diminished. A lot of the environments we live in are comprised mostly of negative strokes. The rule is, "We only pay attention to people when they do something wrong."

The way to motivate people to keep achieving well is to acknowledge what is good, what is already working for them. This is true of children, mates, employees, bosses.

If you haven't had time to read some of the management best sellers in the last five years, let me sum them up for you. Ken Blanchard, The One Minute Manager, said to find someone doing something approximately right and positively acknowledge him for it. Tom Peters, In Search of Excellence, said the companies that are doing the best are the ones that invest in their people. All of the information points to the same outcome: people want positive acknowledgement and will work hard to get it.

What you pay attention to is what you get more of. What you choose to focus on is what will grow. This is the most basic tenet of behavior modification.

Most of us have had the experience of having a small child bring us their drawings for our inspection. What we do is look at the drawings and say something like, "This is a beautiful drawing. I'm going to put it on the refrigerator so everyone will see it!" Within ten minutes we are presented with twenty other drawings! All of us want positive strokes.

A stroke economy is based on these things.

1) Giving strokes.
2) Receiving strokes.
3) Asking for strokes.
4) Saying NO to strokes you don't want.

**Giving strokes:** If you are committing to a positive stroke economy, go home to your family and tell them what is good about them. The most nurturing kind of stroke is about who they ARE, not just what they DO. This is where a child's self-esteem is formed, being told he is a neat kid, irrespective of whether he has just pleased you by performing some task. In our society it is easy to hug and appreciate small children, but somehow we stop doing it as they get older. That's too bad, because teenagers, grown-ups, elderly parents all need positive strokes acutely.

**Receiving strokes** means allowing positive strokes to come in. A lot of people are trained to deflect appreciation ("Oh, no, it wasn't that good a meal, I didn't put enough salt in the gravy.") It is easy to discount the positive — not to hear it, not to allow it in. Even in the midst of abundance, you can starve to death if you will not allow yourself to be nourished. Right now, give yourself permission to allow yourself the kind of pleasure that comes from letting positive strokes in.

**Asking for the strokes you need** is simple enough, though for some people it is not so easy. If you have had a tiring day — or a great day — call up a friend on Friday night and say, "Let's go out to dinner, let's go out and talk. I've missed you." Ask for attention and strokes, and gather people in your life who will give them to you.

**Say no to strokes you don't want.** If someone is giving you mixed messages, or telling you something negative that you think is inappropriate, be willing to preserve your own integrity by saying, "I don't want that. I don't want to be treated that way." It may be scary the first few times, but that is how you can protect your stroke economy and keep yourself fueled with fairness and positive energy. This is not to say that you discount someone's genuine complaint, only that you preserve your right to be treated in a respectful manner.

## THE EMOTIONAL BANK ACCOUNT

Steven Covey talks about an "emotional bank account" that everyone establishes with everyone else. This bank account uses emotional acknowledgements as the currency, not money. Deposits are measured in friendly morning hello's, calling someone on the phone, hugs, sending flowers or remembering birthdays. Anything that shows someone you care.

Obviously, we all want to have high emotional bank balances with people we care about. The higher the deposit side, the more we'll have to draw on when we need to make a withdrawal.

## SAME-SEX SUPPORT

In our life struggles we need support not only from our intimate partners but also from friends of the same sex. This same-sex support is crucial in promoting and protecting our intimate relationships.

Jim Miller, M.A., and Eleanor Greenlee, M.A., in their presentation at the Northwest Bioenergetic Conference explained this need.

"As we grow up we need to separate from the parent of the opposite sex. This usually happens in adolescence. At age twelve or thirteen, when a boy tries to separate from his mother, he'll turn to his father for support.

"If his father isn't available for that support, then the boy is left with mother. The boy is then faced with an identification problem. He needs his father to be supportive of his identity as an emerging young man. If his father isn't there he's in trouble, because his mother is the only person he's getting support from and he needs to separate from her. That's almost impossible to accomplish. We all need support too badly to separate from the main person who is giving us our support.

"This boy then has a problem of identity. He needs a father to show him how to be a man. His father isn't there for him so he learns his emotional attitudes from his mother. (The same is true of girls, just switch the gender.)

"The problem with this shows up most obviously in later life in intimate relationships. If a boy doesn't have father's back-up and support he can't fully separate from mother. He then attempts to separate from the women in his life by developing equivocating and corrective behavior."

You'll see these behaviors in couples all the time. The wife says, "That's a lovely blue sofa." The husband responds, "It's really not a true blue, it's got gray in it." He corrects her and subtly tells her she isn't accurate. The problem with this exacting behavior is when it's chronic. When a man needs to separate from his mother he becomes evaluative and corrective of the current woman in his life. This behavior drives her crazy. She can't do anything right or please him. This pattern is prevalent in both sexes when there is incomplete separation from the parent of the opposite sex.

What needs to happen is to be able to openly disagree and say "no" to your partner. The problem is you can't do that if you don't feel support for your identity from the same sex. You'll be too afraid of losing the support you have from your intimate partner. You can become slick, devious, and hostile, but you don't admit your hostility. Something happens and instead of just being mad, you deny the anger (out of fear) and become very unreasonable.

If this scenario sounds too familiar, you need more resources for personal support than your intimate partner. You need good loving friends of the same sex. As Jim Miller said, "I realized that a great deal of the battling and conflict I had with my first wife had little to do with her but was my attempt to finish my separation from my mother. When I realized this, I called her and apologized for some of my reactions. I have not learned when I'm in a battle with a woman to go to my male friends for support."

The need for same-sex support is fundamental in maintaining intimate relationships with the opposite sex. You can't get from your partner the acknowledgement or separateness or identity that you need. You can't always get your separate opinion supported because sometimes it's in opposition to your partner's opinion. Your partner can't support your identity, at least in heterosexual relationships, because he/she doesn't know what it feels like to be a woman or a man.

The only solution is to turn to a friend of the same sex and build a support system.

For many years I have run support groups for women. These groups meet weekly. Over the course of one year the members in one group each accomplished a personal goal. Marci lost a great deal of weight. Pat got out of a negative job. Nancy became aware of her marketability as a salesperson and increased her income. Beth started her own business.

All of their Deserve Levels were increased rapidly because of the combined energy of group support.

## SUPPORT AND SUCCESS: JESSE'S STORY

Jesse was a fifth-grader living in Missouri. Jesse's year began with his father being taken to prison for writing a number of invalid checks to try to feed his family. Jesse was left at home with his mother and three sisters. His job was to come home after school and take care of his sisters — fix their dinner, help them get their homework done, and get them bathed and put to bed. His mother worked three jobs just to put food on the table and keep a roof over their heads.

Jesse was very responsible. He took care of those little sisters without complaining, but it was a hard time for him. He didn't feel good about himself. He missed his father, he only got to see his mom for about fifteen minutes between her jobs, and frankly, he was depressed.

He didn't have any friends, because when the other kids were playing, Jesse was home taking care of the smaller kids. At age ten he was, in essence, a single parent.

Jesse went to school every day and sat on the back row and looked down at the floor. He didn't interact with the other kids — he didn't know what to say, so he gave up trying.

But he had a teacher who believed in Jesse and supported his growth. Every day as she was working with the kids, Mrs. Skogan would put her hand on his shoulder and say, "Jesse, how're you doing? What can I do for you today?" And he knew that she loved him. She was the only person that whole year who touched him, and that touch made all the difference.

Jesse knew that Mrs. Skogan held a high value on education, and he would have done anything for her approval. He got out of fifth grade, then sixth grade, and finally all the way through high school

— which was amazing, because he had a lot of pressure from home to leave school and go make money.

Jesse even went through two years of college. He started a manufacturing firm and did phenomenally well.

Twenty-five years later, Jesse went back to that classroom and he sat in his old chair again. He watched Mrs. Skogan do what she did so well, which was to love those kids and believe in them.

At the end of the class, he said to her, "You probably don't remember me, but I'm Jesse, and you saved my life. Your love and your support changed what I would have done with myself. I came back to thank you."

With that, he handed her an envelope. Inside it was a check for $50,000. He said, "I want you to know that all the love, all the caring, all the support always comes back."

**So it is with all of us. If you will allow yourself to believe that you deserve the best, that belief will help achieve it — not only for you, but for everyone you come in contact with. By helping each other reach a higher level of deserving, we can change the world, one person at a time.**

# Index

## A



## B



## C,D



## E,F

## G,H,J,K,L,M



## P



## R



## S

## T,U,V,W

# *Give your group a boost!*

With more than fifteen years experience as a psychotherapist, Pat Pearson offers her audiences a wealth of insight. She presents more than 100 seminars a year for companies like IBM, Century 21, RE/MAX, the National Association of Broadcasters, the General Agents and Manager's Conference, Meeting Planners International and Hallmark.

Pat is a leading expert in personal development, sales psychology, employee productivity and business communications.

She was appointed by former Texas Governor Mark White to be a member of the Texas State Speakers Bureau and was selected to be in Who's Who in American Women.

She has entertained and informed audiences from St. John's, Newfoundland to Honolulu, Hawaii and prestigious companies like Century 21, Hallmark and the National Association of Temporary Services have hired her to do national tours.

She is a popular guest on radio and television talk shows.

# *Quotes*

"Learning to understand your deserve level is the most significant achievement you will ever make to guarantee your success. Apply the new techniques in this book to guarantee a successful and exciting life."

Peter H. Thomas, Founder of Century 21 Canada
Chairman of the advisory committee of the
Young Entrepreneurs Organization.

"In my personal experiences with test pilots and astronauts, it is clear that overcoming self-sabotage is a critical component in peak performance. This book can help you achieve that kind of performance."

James S. Logan M.D., M.S., former chief of
Medical Operations N.A.S.A. Johnson Space
Center

"If you have postponed happiness or prevented your dreams from becoming reality, you need this book. Your life is not a dress rehearsal and here is your opportunity to learn how to get out of your own way."

Peter McGugan, best selling author of "Beating Burnout:
the survival guide for the 90s" and "When Something
Changes Everything".

"This is a practical guide to overcoming self-sabotage. Pat gives a clear description of the relationship between a positive self image and success".

Harville Hendrix, Best selling author of
"Getting The Love You Want"